John

Student Edition

CROSSROADS SERIES

Produced under the auspices of the
North American Division of Seventh-day Adventists
Office of Education

Published by
Pacific Press® Publishing Association
Nampa, Idaho

2008

Contents

Your Religion Class

This section provides you with some general information about the CROSSROADS SERIES and your religion class.

THE CROSSROADS SERIES

The CROSSROADS SERIES contains the religion curriculum for Seventh-day Adventist secondary schools, grades 9-12. This textbook is a part of the series.

LOGO OF THE CROSSROADS SERIES

The logo of the CROSSROADS SERIES symbolizes the underlying theme of the series—that the Cross of Jesus Christ is at the very center of the Christian faith. God's revelation of Himself in the Cross reveals the only sacrifice for sin and the ultimate significance of life to each person and to every nation. Thus the Cross stands as the decisive moment of truth for all humankind through all ages. The logo, in symbolic form, portrays the centrality of the Cross with all paths (roads) of human experience and personal decisions leading to and from it.

GOAL OF THE CROSSROADS SERIES

The goal of the CROSSROADS SERIES is to lead young people to the loving and redeeming God of Scripture. His self-revelation has its focus and fulfillment in the life, death, resurrection, and intercession of Jesus Christ, whose substitutionary death on the cross is the sole basis of Christian assurance. With Christ as Savior and Lord, each believer is enabled, through the Holy Spirit, to experience a life of worship, growth, and service, and to proclaim and stand ready for His return.

UNITS OF STUDY GRADES 11, 12

There are ten units of study that comprise the religion curriculum for grades 11, 12. Each unit is published in a separate textbook. The units of study (textbooks) are:

Daniel and Revelation
Beliefs
Friendships
Romans
Choices and Challenges
Hebrews
Marriage and Family
Worldviews and Religion
Life Philosophy and Moral Issues
John

VERSIONS OF THE HOLY BIBLE USED IN THE CROSSROADS SERIES

The NEW INTERNATIONAL VERSION, referred to as NIV, is used as the primary version of Scripture for the Anchor Text, scriptural references quoted in the narrative section of the lesson, and answers to Bible Search activities and Practical Application. Other versions of Scripture have also been used when the particular version enriches the meaning of a given reference.

MEMORIZATION OF SCRIPTURE

Each lesson contains a verse labeled Anchor Text. Some or all of these verses will be assigned to memorize. The content of the references should first be understood, both as to their meaning and their application to your life.

Dear Student,

You are about to begin a journey that could change your life!

For the next few weeks, you will be doing much more than just studying the Gospel According to John. This Bible class has a unique approach since it is both devotional and academic.

You will find this journey more valuable if you invest the time and effort that are an integral part of the devotional focus of this class. An important part of your devotional experience will be journaling—keeping a kind of spiritual diary.

Some of the great thinkers and leaders of the past have acknowledged that journaling plays a rewarding role in discovering personal fulfillment in life.

This unit has many elements that involve reflection, prayer, and other devotional experiences. Even if it feels uncomfortable at first, take these opportunities to reach out and grow. In time, you may discover how much these experiences have enriched your life.

Allow God to lead you past the academic aspects of studying the book of John in order to meet Jesus in an intensely personal way. He invites you to walk with Him as you journey together.

Principles of a Devotional Life

Relationships between people are grounded on three things: talking, listening, and doing things together. The same basic dynamics are crucial to a relationship with Jesus. If we wish to have a relationship with Jesus, we need to spend time talking with Him, listening to Him, and doing things together with Him. Related to each lesson in this unit will be opportunities to practice these three dynamics. Here we will summarize some of the key principles of a devotional relationship with Jesus.

Talking to Jesus

The basic means of talking to Jesus is prayer. Yet many Christians of all ages have struggled to make prayer work for them. How can it be different for you?

1. **Be flexible.** Don't be locked into any particular position in which to pray; in other words, it is unimportant whether or not you are on your knees, whether your eyes are open or shut, whether you fold your hands or put them behind your back or raise them up in the air. A careful look at the prayers described in the Bible indicate that there is no one right position for prayer; the right position for you is the one that best helps you connect with God. For some, silent prayer is more effective with the eyes open and focused on some object, such as the pattern of a bedspread or couch.

2. **Try writing out some of your prayers.** (The prayer questions in the various lessons of this unit will encourage you to practice this.) It is amazing what the process of writing does to help concentrate your mind on the reality of being in the act of prayer. Take a notebook and a pencil or a pen, sit down, and construct a carefully worded prayer to God. Computer wizards may find a computer the most effective way to do this.

3. **Be relevant.** When you pray, focus on the things that truly matter to you. One reason that prayer may sometimes seem irrelevant to everyday life is that the crucial elements of everyday life are not brought forward to God while in the attitude of prayer. Discuss with God the very things that are of utmost concern to you at a given time.

4. **Thank God in very specific ways.** Thank Him for air, water, the color of the carpet, the animal you just saw out of the window. This may seem a bit silly at first, but where would you be without air? What would life be like without color, without animals? Who made these things? If you feel so depressed that you can't come up with anything to be thankful for, get out a dictionary—it's loaded with names of gifts from God. Just open any page, and you will find them: apes, apples, apricots, and so on. When was the last time you thanked the Lord for those things?

Yes, I know this sounds like the most childish thing you have ever heard. But I want you to know something—it works. The Bible says, "The joy of the Lord is your strength" (Nehemiah 8:10). The best way to find the joy of the Lord is through a spirit of gratitude and praise. The best way to develop such an attitude is to learn to thank God for everything you receive.

Listening to Jesus

How do you listen to Someone whose voice you cannot hear? The primary method, of course, is to hear Jesus' voice in Scripture. A major theme of the Gospel of John is that Jesus' words in the written Gospel (as well as the rest of the Bible) are as powerful and effective as His spoken words and physical touch were to those who knew Him in the flesh.

How can Scripture study bring us into a living relationship with Jesus?

1. **Choose relevant readings.** To be devotionally useful, reading must be relevant to present experience, to things that matter in practical terms. What are the greatest concerns and needs in your life? To center study on matters of lesser concern would certainly be a mistake. Genealogies and prophecies may be of intense intellectual interest, but they may not offer practical guidance for the daily issues of the school, home, work, and the neighborhood.

2. **Focus on Jesus.** Since a personal knowledge of Jesus Christ is the most relevant of all spiritual concerns, devotional study needs to focus on Jesus. The Gospel of

John is far more relevant to this purpose than 1 Chronicles or Judges, for example. The other Gospels, letters of Paul and, for Adventist youth, books such as *The Desire of Ages* and *Steps to Christ,* by Ellen G. White, can be particularly helpful.

3. **Take your time.** In devotional reading, the most important thing is to discern God's voice to you personally, not to accomplish the task of completing a certain number of pages or mastering a certain amount of information. If it takes a whole hour to meditate on one sentence, so be it. The devotional life is not the time and place to rush. Take your time; go no farther or faster than you are able to understand what you've been reading. Allow the reading to sink in—let it impact the very core of your being.

4. **Write out special insights.** Write down or enter into your computer the "highlight-film" kind of insights that God gives you as part of your devotional experience. People forget what they don't write down. The most effective devotional book that you could read might be your personal record of spiritual discoveries. These insights will help you to rekindle your walk with Jesus in tough times. The

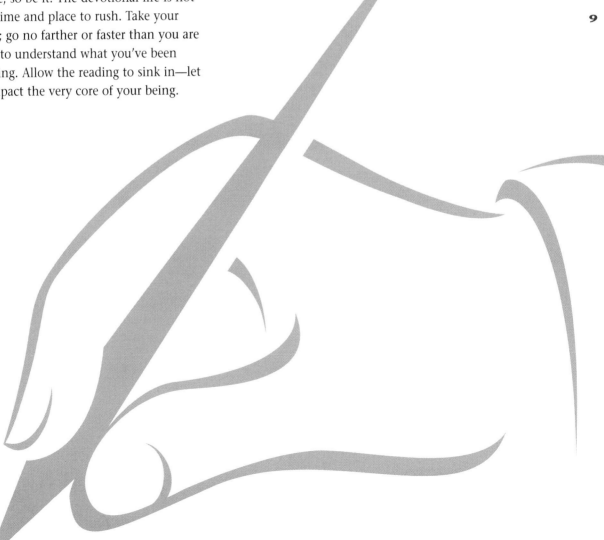

Insight questions in the various lessons of this unit will encourage you to practice this.

5. **Keep a spiritual diary** of struggles, experiences, and dialogues with God in the course of your life. Don't limit yourself to devotional note-taking. Challenge your experience with God, ask Him direct questions like, "How do you feel about my friendships right now and about the way I relate to my parents? What are my most important needs right now? How would You want me to meet them? Am I being sensitive to Your leading in my life right now?" Experience questions can be found in every lesson.

Most of us take very little time to reflect on our lives. But the fact of the matter is, if you don't keep score of your life, you will repeat the same errors over and over again. If every day we would take time to sit down and reflect on the previous day and ask, "Did I give glory to God?" there would be an amazing growth of self-awareness. We would begin to see things in ourselves that everyone who knows us can see, but we are blinded to ourselves.

6. **Let God answer your prayers.** There is another exciting aspect of listening to Jesus. When you have finished praying, stay on your knees. Put a notebook in front of you, pick up your pencil, and wait. You have talked to God about the things that matter most. You have asked for His presence with you. You are now in a position to receive. So write down whatever comes to mind. Do not try to evaluate it at once; treat this as spiritual brainstorming.

Working Together With Jesus

Without concrete and practical faith-action, however, the study and prayer life can easily become confined to a closet separate from the rest of a person's experience. What happens in the devotional life will have little impact on everyday experience, unless accompanied by conscious, corresponding action. How you live has a powerful effect on your sense of God's presence in your life.

This class in the Gospel of John focuses directly on the study-and-prayer aspects of a living relationship with God. But the following ideas are part of a balanced walk that can easily be incorporated into your overall academy experience.

1. **Sharing faith is not an option.**
   Expression deepens impression. Talk faith

and you will have more faith. Whenever the Cross of Christ is uplifted, the Holy Spirit presses the claim of the Cross home with power to whomever is listening. But that same power spills back to the one who testifies. Sharing your faith with others strengthens and confirms your own faith. And when you live out your care and concern for the lost, you participate in Jesus' care for them, which draws you closer to His heart.

2. **Stretch the limits.** Don't be afraid to do something radical with God. Do a short-term mission project in a part of the world much different from yours. (This doesn't have to be overseas; you could go to inner-city America if you grew up on a farm or to rural America if you grew up in a city.) Plant a garden, dedicate a portion as a special gift to God, and see what happens. Spend time getting to know public-high-school students, seeking ways to interest them in deeper values. Shared risk enhances intimacy with others. Risking yourself for God enhances intimacy with God.

3. **Walk the talk.** How you live has a powerful impact on what you believe. This is why evangelists like to call people up front. There is something about getting out of your seat and walking to the front that nails down a decision in a way that very few other things can do. Action has a powerful impact on belief and experience.

Relationship with Jesus is most powerfully affirmed as part of a seven-day-a-week experience, one that impacts in some way on every moment of every day of our lives.

While the term "Adventist lifestyle" may mean different things to different people, it can be an important part of living together with Jesus every day. For example, when an Adventist shops for clothes, the question is, "What impact will this clothing have on my witness for Christ? Will it aid or hinder my mission in life?" When an Adventist shops for groceries, time is spent reading labels. Why? Because there is a desire to not put into the body things that will clog up the mind and render the individual less fit for the difficult task of honoring God in all that is done, said, or thought. These are just two of many ways we can constantly be reminded of Jesus' claim on our life.

There are dangers in two extremes. A rigid lifestyle without a living relationship with God is drudgery. But a devotional life without practice is also doomed to fail. Finding the balance between the two extremes can be both challenging and exciting! And in the process Jesus becomes more real to us.

4. **Act on impressions.** After the spiritual brainstorming mentioned in the previous section, test the ideas that came to your mind. Some may be from God, others, from the fog of your internal dreams and/or confusion. But as you prayerfully consider these impressions, you will gradually become able to discern when it is God speaking to you in your mind and when it is not.

His word is as good as His touch.

Lesson 1

Walking With Jesus in the Gospel of John

Lesson Setting

This opening lesson takes on the dual purpose of this unit's lessons: to help develop a working knowledge of the Gospel of John and a living relationship with the Jesus of this Gospel. The lesson, therefore, offers some basic principles of a devotional relationship with Jesus in the context of the unique features of this Gospel.

W ow, is she ever beautiful!" "What a personality!" "The man of my dreams!" "It doesn't get any better than this!" "I've never been so happy in my life!"

What is it like when young people fall in love? I remember one of my first experiences with love when I was in the academy back home in the big city. I had no illusions that she was the most beautiful girl in the world, but she sure looked beautiful to me! Not knowing how she felt about me at first, I consulted with people who knew her and found out where she lived and how she traveled to school. I then went out of my way to hang around certain subway platforms, just to catch a glimpse of her as she went by on her way home from school.

I would find excuses to attend her church instead of my own. I would watch for her in the halls between classes. I could sense when she had entered a crowded room long before I saw her. When I learned that she cared as much about me as I did about her, finding time with her became the highest priority of my school day.

The best block of time was on the way home. Although I lived an hour and a half away in another state (first subway, then bus), I would ride with her on the subway, all the way to her station, even though it was quite a bit out of the way. Sometimes we would buy time for conversation by letting three, four, even six or seven trains pass before boarding one on the way to her place. Everything took second place to finding time to be together.

Relationship is all about being together, spending time with each other, talking and listening, and doing things together. When you love someone, you want to spend time

Have you ever observed a good friend fall in love? In what ways did your friend change as a person? How did his or her use of time change?

How do you have a relationship with someone you can't see or hear or touch?

with that person. According to the Gospel of John, the most important relationship you will ever have is the one you form with Jesus. The purpose of this Gospel is to help people fall in love with Jesus and to show them how to spend time with Him, even though they can't see, hear, or touch Him directly.

Journaling
(Experience)

What is the highest priority in my life right now? The second highest? If I were to meet Jesus face to face, would He be pleased by these priorities? Why?

Journaling
(Prayer)

Invite Jesus to reprioritize your life according to His Word.

Bible Search
Knowing God

Answer the following questions on the basis of the texts provided:

1. According to the Gospel of John, what is the basis for eternal life? John 17:3.
2. How is relationship with Jesus described in John 15:1-8?
3. Where was Jesus "in the beginning"? John 1:1, 2.
4. How is Jesus' relationship with His Father described in John 1:18?
5. How close is Jesus to God the Father? John 14:9.

The key to eternal life is to know Jesus, to have a relationship with Him. Why? Because according to the Gospel of John,

Jesus had, and continues to have, the most intimate of relationships with God the Father. He knows God; He is God. But the Gospel tells how Jesus came down to this earth not only to show human beings what God is like, but to offer a real, living relationship with God to the human race. To know Jesus is to know God. To know God is to have eternal life.

In the Gospel of John, then, the key to Christian experience is to get to know Jesus personally, to become His friend, to live with Him, talk to Him, and experience Him. When we do this, we are brought into intimate relationship with God. We can be as close to God as branches are to the vine.

The big problem is, how do you do that in a secular world? *How do you have a relationship with someone you can't see or hear or touch?* How do you know Jesus when the fleeting images of television or the Internet sometimes seem more real than God? That, above all else, is a question this Gospel was uniquely designed to answer.

Bible Search
His Word Is as Good as His Touch

Answer the following questions on the basis of the texts provided:

6. What is the twofold purpose of the Gospel as expressed in John 20:30, 31?
7. What two types of belief are mentioned in John 20:29?
8. What did Thomas feel he needed to have before he could believe in Jesus? John 20:24-28.
9. How often did Jesus touch people while performing the following miracles?

John 2:1-11; 4:46-54; 5:1-14; 9:1-7; 11:38-44.

10. For what group did Jesus offer a special prayer? John 17:20.

This group includes every generation since the time of John. Jesus not only prayed for His disciples, but He prayed for us as well.

Have you ever felt that those who knew Jesus in the flesh had an advantage over us today? Have you ever felt that it would be easier to be a Christian if Jesus lived next

Have you ever felt that it would be easier to be a Christian if Jesus lived next door and you could talk to Him face to face?

door and you could talk to Him face to face? The same concern was felt by the generation to whom the Gospel of John was written.

The Fourth Gospel was written in the context of the impending death of the "beloved disciple," who was the last living link with those who had known Jesus in the flesh—the first Christian generation. John's death threatened to plunge the second generation of Christians into confusion and uncertainty. What would become of them without the guidance of those who had known and talked to Jesus in person?

The Gospel's statement of purpose (John 20:30, 31) follows the "doubting Thomas"

story of John 20:24-29. In verse 29 Jesus says, "Because you have seen me, you have believed; blessed are those who have not seen and yet have believed." Thomas here represents all of the disciples, the first generation, those who have seen and touched Jesus, while Jesus' statement reaches out to the second generation, who have been denied that privilege. Evidently seeing and personal contact are not crucial to the development of faith. The difference between the disciples and the original readers of the Gospel was that the disciples' faith was based on seeing, while that of the readers was not. And the greater blessing was pronounced on the second generation, those who came to faith apart from physical contact with Jesus. We are part of that generation, Christians who have no physical contact with Jesus or with anyone who knew Him in the flesh.

That brings us to the question that led us into this study. How do you develop a relationship with Jesus when you can't see Him, hear Him, or touch Him? The Gospel of John was written specifically to answer that question. The answer is clearly seen when one compares the miracles of Jesus in the Fourth Gospel with those in Matthew, Mark, and Luke. In each of the other Gospels, Jesus repeatedly uses touch in performing His miracles (Matthew 8:3, 4; 8:14, 15; 9:18-25; 9:29, 30; 14:29-31; 20:34; Mark 1:29-31; 1:40-42; 5:21-43; 7:31-35; 8:22-26; 9:25-27; Luke 4:40; 5:12, 13; 7:14, 15; 8:40-56; 13:10-13; 22:50, 51). But in the Gospel of John, such touching is remarkably absent.

At the wedding at Cana (2:1-11), the

water is turned into wine without any physical contact on Jesus' part. The royal official's son in Capernaum is healed by Jesus in Cana, some sixteen miles away from Capernaum (4:46-54)! Jesus does not touch the paralytic at the pool of Bethesda (5:1-15). In chapter 9 He smears a little clay into the blind man's eyes, but the miracle does not take place until the man washes his eyes in the Pool of Siloam, more than a kilometer away (9:6, 7). In chapter 11 Lazarus is called from the tomb; Jesus does not need to shake him or drag him out first. A common

His word is as good as His touch.

denominator of all these "signs" is the lack of physical contact in performing the miracle. Distance is evidently no barrier to the reception of Jesus' blessings. We can conclude, therefore, that the second generation's lack of personal contact with Jesus placed them at no disadvantage.

It is also a fact that each of the miracles mentioned above is accomplished by the words of Jesus. To the servants at the wedding at Cana, He says, "Fill" and "draw" (2:7, 8). To the royal official, He says, "You may go. Your son will live" (4:50). To the paralytic, He says, "Get up! Pick up your mat and walk" (5:8). To the blind man, He says, "Go" and "wash" (9:7). To Lazarus He says, "Come out!" (11:43). In each case it is the words of Jesus that accomplish His intention, not His physical touch.

For the second generation, the message that comes through in these scenes is the power of Jesus' words to overcome barriers of space. *His word is as good as His touch!* His

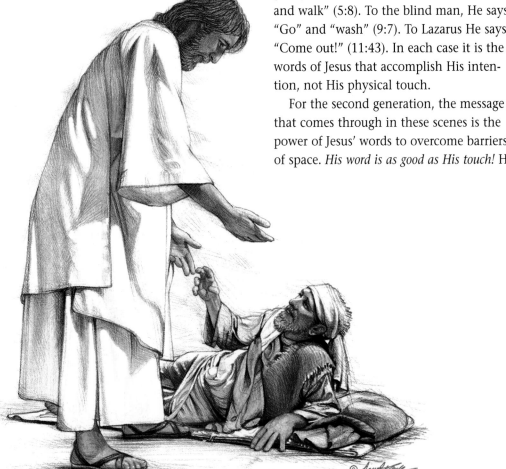

word is as powerful at a distance as it is close at hand. Though only ministered through a printed page, it still retains its power to save and to heal. It is through that Word that the Holy Spirit ministers to the needs of the second generation (14:26, 27).

We share in the second generation's deficiency. We, too, would love to have the privilege of Thomas, whose faith was fully confirmed by sight. We, too, would appreciate a face-to-face relationship with Jesus. But the Gospel of John tells us that the seeming absence of God in our time is no barrier to the mighty working of Jesus through the Spirit. *His word is as good as His touch.* The benefits that were available through the physical ministry of Jesus are now available through His word! The Gospel also teaches us how to gain those benefits. In each of the miracle stories, some human party had to carry out the words of Jesus in order for the miracle to take place. The servants had to pour water before they could draw wine, the paralytic had to arise and gather his bedding, the blind man had to go to the Pool of Siloam and wash.

The implicit message to the reader of the Gospel is twofold. (1) The reader must know the words of Jesus and discern their application to his or her particular situation. The careful study of this Gospel is the great living replacement for the face-to-face relationship that the disciples had with Jesus. (2) The reader must carry out what Jesus commands. The power of Jesus through the Spirit accompanies actions in obedience to His words. The Fourth Gospel was written so that those who had not seen might believe

(20:29-31). It is by reading and applying the Gospel that believers today obtain the life that Jesus shared when He was physically on this earth. This theme makes the Gospel of John the ideal starting point for a devotional relationship with Jesus.

 ## Journaling for Your Spiritual Diary

Gain "insight" by crafting a thoughtful response to the following questions:

How does John's message to the second generation affect your understanding of relationship with Jesus today? Is it encouraging to know that Jesus prayed for you? Why?

John's Unique Picture of Jesus

Before we close this lesson, a number of unique elements in the Gospel of John are worthy of attention.

1. The Jesus of the Fourth Gospel is not the "lowly Jesus, meek and mild" of the Synoptics. He is assertive (3:3; 4:17, 18, 48; 5:45-47; 7:6-9), combative (3:10-12; 5:39, 40, 42, 44; 8:44), seems to enjoy the rough and tumble of debate (3:1-15; 8:31-47), and may even be purposefully sarcastic at times (9:41; 10:32). Yet He always speaks the truth in love, even if it has to be tough love.

2. Most of the stories in John are not found in the other three gospels. Particularly noteworthy are the extended one-on-one encounters between Jesus and various individuals in the Gospel; Nicodemus (3:1-21), the Samaritan woman (4:4-42), the paralytic at Bethesda (5:1-15), the blind man

(9:1-41), Pilate (18:28–19:16), and Peter (21:15-23).

3. Although parables play a major role in Jesus' ministry in Matthew, Mark, and Luke, they are rare and by some definitions nonexistent in the Gospel of John. The closest you come to parables in the Fourth Gospel are the allegories of the Good Shepherd (10:1-18) and the True Vine (15:1-8). But these are not true parables according to the pattern found in the other three gospels.

4. In Matthew, Mark, and Luke, Jesus visits Jerusalem only once during His ministry, which is focused mainly on Galilee. In John, however, Jesus repeatedly visits Jerusalem, and His ministry makes a much bigger impact on Jerusalem and Judea. Although these visits are not mentioned in the other three Gospels, they are implied in a couple of Jesus' statements (Matthew 23:37; Luke 13:34).

5. Unlike Matthew, Mark, and Luke, and

Reaction

Discussion Questions

1. Are there times in life when you don't want to be with people you love? What kinds of things make you feel that way?

2. Can you envision a situation in which it would be OK not to want to spend time with Jesus? Why?

3. What is the relationship between knowing Jesus and obedience to His will?

4. What kinds of things make a distance relationship worth maintaining? In what ways do letters, phone calls, and e-mail prepare the way for face-to-face encounter?

5. Why was it so hard for Thomas to believe, based only on the reports of his friends? In what ways was Thomas like us?

6. Why is it that seeing Jesus turn water into wine or raising Lazarus from the dead produced less faith than the written stories about those miracles?

7. How do you think your life would be different if Jesus lived next door? Would your friends more likely be impressed or turned off by His behavior? Why?

8. How could various writers portray Jesus so differently? Does that make you more or less likely to accept that their accounts are truthful? Why?

very unlike the book of Revelation, written by the same author, the Gospel of John has little emphasis on the future end of the world at the second coming of Jesus. Instead, it focuses on the heavenlike joys of a relationship with Jesus in the here and now. Eternal life (John 5:24, 25), the judgment (John 3:18-21; 12:31), the resurrection (John 5:24, 25), and face-to-face encounter with God (John 1:18; 14:9)—things that are described as future in the other biblical books—all become present realities in the person and work of Jesus. John is not denying these future realities; he simply wants to emphasize the fullness of what the second generation can experience because it has the words of Jesus.

Anchor Text

"This is eternal life: that they may know you, the only true God, and Jesus Christ, whom you have sent" (John 17:3).

Expanded Horizons

Look up each of the following passages in the Gospel: John 21:1-14; 15:1-7; 17:1-26; 10:1-21; 1:35-51; 20:1-18. What person(s) or element in each story (passage) represents the second generation of Christians—those who had no personal contact with Jesus but came to faith through the words and actions of others?

In a paragraph describe the collective role you think these persons or elements played in the message of the Gospel.

CREATIVE PROJECTS

Five major miracles in the Gospel of John (John 2:1-11; 4:46-54; 5:1-14; 9:1-7; 11:38-44) are remarkable in that Jesus avoids touch in performing each miracle. John selected these miracles to express the theme that Jesus' word was as good as His touch or His physical presence. This encouraged the second generation of Christians at a time when they were losing the last living disciple of Jesus. Create a poster, mural, clay model, or even a series of cartoon sketches that illustrate one of the above miracle stories.

Jesus challenged the walls of religious exclusiveness.

Lesson 2

Jesus Is the Best

Lesson Setting

Scripture: John 1:1-51.

One of the most magnificent passages in the Bible is the Prologue to the Gospel of John (John 1:1-18). Here Jesus is portrayed as the Word who was God being made flesh and then returning to the Father's side. The rest of chapter 1 focuses on John the Baptist as the one who points out Jesus and initiates a succession of disciples who join Him.

H ave you ever seen a cricket or some other type of insect in church? Have you ever wondered what its life was like? How it viewed its world?

There is one thing you and I have in common with a cricket—limited vision. None of us does too well imagining life beyond the limits of what we can see and experience. You see, as far as the cricket in church is concerned, his entire universe is an auditorium. Can you see him taking his daughter out at night and telling her to look up at the ceiling? He strokes her wing with one of his front legs and sighs, "It's a mighty big sky we live under, girl." Does he know that he sees only a fraction of the world?

Crickets have limited hopes and dreams. A cricket's highest dream is to find a piece of bread. He falls asleep amid visions of pie crumbs and jam drippings. Or consider the hero of the cricket's world. Crickets cheer for the most talented members of their species. A fast one who dashes across a room full of feet without being squashed. A gutsy one who has explored the hinterland of the baptistry. A courageous one who has ventured to the edge of a mighty cabinet or hopped along the precipice of a windowsill.

Who do you suppose a cricket worships, anyway? Does she acknowledge that there was a creative hand behind the construction of the church she lives in? Or does she choose to worship the building itself? Or perhaps a particular place within the building? Does she assume that since she has never seen the builder, there was no builder?

Perhaps some crickets become intellectually advanced and engage in philosophical questions such as, "Is there life beyond the auditorium?" Some crickets believe there is. There must be a creator of the place. How else would the lights come on?

> If Jesus were a teenager growing up in your hometown and attending your Bible class, what do you think He would be like? Would He be very different from the rest of the class? If so, in what ways? What do you think His favorite food would be? His favorite hobby? How would your spiritual life be different with Him in the class?

How else could air blow through the vents? How else could music fill the room? Out of amazement for what they can see, they worship what they can't see and can't explain.

Other crickets disagree. They explain that the lights come on because of electricity, the air blows because of air conditioners, and music is the result of stereos and speakers. "There is no life beyond this room," they declare. "All we have to do is figure out how

If we have never seen the hand that made the universe, may we assume that there is no life beyond the here and now?

everything works."

Many humans are satisfied living with similar limits. If we have never seen the hand that made the universe, we may assume that there is no life beyond the here and now. We may believe that there is no truth beyond what we can experience on this limited planet. We may assume that there is no purpose beyond our own pleasure. Nothing eternal. No divine factor in existence. Like a cricket that refuses to acknowledge a builder, we may refuse to acknowledge our Creator.

In light of this, John 1 tells an amazing story. It is as if the builder of the church became a cricket and entered the church to help the crickets understand a far greater reality than they could possibly grasp on the basis of their limited vision. In the prologue to John, we catch a glimpse beyond our limited "room" and touch base with the Creator Himself! And wonder of wonders, the Creator Himself came down and walked among us, learned our language, and showed us in human terms what God is like. This could be the most important revelation of reality anyone could possibly have. This Gospel could be our best chance of escaping the narrow world of limited perception into the vast universe of ultimate reality!

Journaling
(Experience)

Explore the limits of your ability to understand God and His ways without the insights of Scripture.

Bible Search
The Word Became Flesh

Read John 1:1-18 and then answer the following questions:

1. How far back in time does the Word go?
2. What relationship did the Word have with God?
3. How do we know that the Word was not a created being?
4. What did Jesus have that every human being needs?
5. What happened to the Word according to John 1:14?
6. To whom is Jesus compared in John 1:15-17?

Journaling

(Insight)

Write out the insights you gain about God as you realize how completely He made Himself available to us in Jesus.

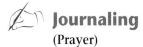

Journaling

(Prayer)

Thank God for allowing Jesus to become one of us at great cost to Himself.

Thank Jesus for being willing to sacrifice His privileges and position to walk among us and show God to us.

Jesus of New York

If Jesus were a teenager growing up in today's world and attending your academy (or would He be home-schooled?), what would He be like? Would He be very different from the rest of the class? If so, in what ways? Would He occasionally sit down and watch TV or a video? Play a computer game? If so, what would His favorites be? Would He play on the football team? Would He have a favorite sports figure? Whom would He like to see become president of the United States or prime minister of Canada? Far more important, what impact would He have on His fellow students and teachers? How would your academy be different because He was there? How would you be different if He lived with you?

The Bible is virtually silent about Jesus' teen years. There is just the cryptic statement in Luke 2:52: "Jesus grew in wisdom and stature, and in favor with God and

men." We learn from this statement that He matured physically, mentally, and spiritually through His teen years and that He was generally appreciated by other people.

The Adventist artist Greg Constantine has produced an exciting series of sketches he entitled "Jesus of New York." He imagines Jesus as a teen, wearing a New York Yankees baseball cap and jeans, encountering a variety of both everyday and unusual situations. In these sketches Constantine tries to fill in the silent years of Jesus' youth, but in a contemporary setting of subway trains, airports, muggings, television, sporting events, and the frantic rough and tumble of urban existence. This is the kind of world in which we need to learn how to live as Jesus would have if He were growing up here and now.

In the book *The Desire of Ages,* Ellen G. White amplifies the meager picture of Luke 2 in a chapter entitled "Days of Conflict." Her description of Jesus as a teen is most interesting.

Independence Based on Principle. As a teen, Jesus grounded His religious experience on principles rather than merely following rules made by others. He did not attack the practices of the leaders in the church; He just submitted His everyday decisions to the principles of the Scriptures. When the leaders reproved Him for not obeying a rule, He always pointed them to the Bible as the justification for His conduct.

Desire to Serve Others. His role, however, was not that of a contentious rebel. He was not different just to be different. He diverged from custom only when obedience to God's Word required it. In a gentle and submissive way, He tried to express kindness to everyone with whom He came in contact. He was tactful in His dealings with people. He was always sympathetic to those who suffered. He helped them carry their burdens, both physical and psychological. He went out of His way to be at peace with everyone, if they would allow Him.

Independence Brings Opposition. But Jesus' gentleness and tact did not mean that He was a doormat who could be swayed by intimidation. Although He was kind toward those who disagreed, He was firm in His biblical principles. This firmness, however, often got Him in trouble with the religious leaders—and even with His family.

He suffered at the hands of His older brothers, who accused Him of stubbornness and of disregarding the faith of their fathers. They accused Jesus of thinking Himself superior to them and to the religious teachers. They tried to intimidate Him. They were both jealous and contemptuous.

Jesus' mother, pressured by His brothers and the religious leaders, strongly urged Him to conform to the practices of the time. She loved Him dearly, but was frustrated by His refusal to conform. It complicated her life to see so much discord in the home, but Jesus' Scripture-based principles did not allow any easy fixes.

Jesus Was Inclusive. One of the main

areas in which Jesus disregarded tradition was its exclusiveness. He was open to relationship with anyone, regardless of their religion or life practice. He cheerfully helped whoever needed help. He would often skip meals to feed people who were more needy than He was. His life was a living demonstration of the gospel in its lack of prejudice toward people of every heritage or background.

Because He challenged the walls of religious exclusiveness, He was often more at home at the margins of society than in the mainstream. Although impatient with His scruples, most people at the margins of the faith enjoyed His presence because He was always cheerful, kind, helpful, and interesting. He taught them that they were endowed by God with precious talents, which could be employed to make a mighty difference in the world. Every moment had great potential for good. He treated no human being as worthless.

Yet even at the margins of society, His life was not easy. While Jesus was never impatient in word or look, He could not witness sin or abuse without pain that was impossible to disguise. Because Jesus' life condemned evil, many retaliated by casting contempt on Him regarding the circumstances of His birth. They would also accuse Him of being too narrow and straitlaced. Jesus was too independent for the religious people and too conscientious for the irreligious.

Jesus' Source of Strength. To cope with these difficulties, Jesus spent significant amounts of time away from people out in nature. There He would contemplate the Scriptures and talk with His Father. Afterward, He would come back refreshed and ready to face whatever life held for that day. If Jesus needed that kind of relationship with God in order to cope, how much more do we need it?

Why should we pay special attention to the life of Jesus? Because the Prologue to John's Gospel teaches us that a teenager in first-century Galilee was greater than Moses, greater than John the Baptist. He was the living representation of the character of God in human flesh. In Jesus we can know what God would be like if He lived among us. In Jesus we are lifted beyond the limitations of human perception to gain a clear grasp of eternity. In Jesus the path to relationship with God is made clear.

 Journaling

(Insight)

What insight did you gain from the section above about Jesus? About your own attempts to follow Him?

 Bible Search

From the Baptist to Jesus

Read John 1:19-51 and then answer the following questions:

7. What act resulted in the first disciples approaching Jesus?
8. Who were the first disciples to follow Jesus?
9. What were the names of the other three disciples who joined Jesus shortly thereafter?
10. In what three ways did Jesus respond to these disciples?
11. What ten titles are applied to Jesus in John 1:29-51?

In John 1:19-51, John shows Jesus, the God-man of the Prologue, the bearer of mighty titles, interacting with everyday people as an adult.

 Anchor Text

"The Word became flesh and made his dwelling among us. We have seen his glory, the glory of the One and Only, who came from the Father, full of grace and truth" (John 1:14).

Reaction

1. Why do you think John begins his Gospel before Creation when all the other Gospels begin either with Jesus' birth or with His adult ministry?

2. If a person knew Jesus in the flesh, would it be easier or harder to believe that Jesus had preexisted as God for all eternity? Why?

3. Why do you think people are so easily satisfied with limited knowledge about God and about reality?

4. Why do you think God sent Jesus to first-century Palestine instead of some other time and place? Would it be easier or harder for Jesus to have an impact on society today? Why?

5. How are teenage attempts to show independence treated in today's world? By adults? By other teenagers? In what ways are youth pressed to conform? In what ways do we avoid expressing independence for fear of opposition?

6. To what degree does the church today reflect the inclusiveness of Jesus? How can we learn to be more inclusive in our own experience? What type of people do we have a hard time including?

7. What does Jesus' need for devotional time with God tell us about our own need for it?

1. There is evidence that the Prologue of John (John 1:1-18) was based on an early Christian hymn. In Greek, the poetic rhythms of a hymn can be detected in verses 1-5, 9-11, 14, and 16-18. Rewrite all or part of the Prologue in poetic form, using your own words. If you have musical ability, put your poem to music and share it with the class. You may want to personalize your poem or song (as if He came down just for you).

2. In John 1:6-8, 15 Jesus is portrayed as superior to John the Baptist. The Baptist appears again in 1:19-37; 3:22-30; 5:33-36; and 10:40-42. List all statements in which the Baptist is deliberately painted in inferior terms. Why do you think the author of this Gospel collected so many negative statements about the Baptist? How does that serve the author's purpose?

 CREATIVE PROJECTS

1. With the help of a concordance, look up and record all the texts in John that mention Moses. How was Moses regarded by the people of the time? What points might John be trying to make comparing Jesus with Moses?

2. Imagine that Jesus had been sent into today's world. Imagine how He would present Himself and how He would react to many contemporary situations. Design a logo that you think would express the essence of Jesus' character and mission.

3. Start a "Be Like Jesus" club at your school (come up with a better name for it too). Challenge your friends and teachers to submit their actions and relationships to the principles of Scripture and the example of Jesus' own teen years. Utilize *The Desire of Ages*, chapter 9, and the insights of this unit to develop principles of life for teenagers in today's world. Then try to carry out those principles day by day. You might consider, for example, creating a baseball cap utilizing a logo created by a club member in response to Project 2. At the end of the unit, write a two- to three-page essay on the trials and the joys of trying to be like Jesus.

Good things can crowd out the best.

Lesson 3

When Change Is for the Better

Lesson Setting

Scripture: John 2:1-22.

This section of the Gospel begins shortly after the time when the Baptist identifies Jesus and helps Him begin to collect disciples. After the wedding at Cana, Jesus goes home to Capernaum for several months and then goes down to Jerusalem at the time of the Passover.

*A*nother day, another shekel. Business *has been going well for a while,* Micah the caterer thought to himself. *Lots of young people growing up, lots of marriages to celebrate, lots of food and drink to prepare.* People needed caterers for such occasions. It was a decent living, and a lot of satisfaction came with it: helping families get together, seeing happy people enjoying a good feast.

This particular wedding was a bit strange, however. Micah had been approached by Mary to cater a wedding for one of her relatives (see *The Desire of Ages,* 146). It was rumored that Mary considered her son Yeshuah to be born of the Holy Spirit (a novel claim for a young, engaged woman who had been caught pregnant!). Another rumor was that perhaps He was the long-hoped-for Messiah. Some people were concerned, therefore, that Yeshuah's arrival with

His disciples would create a sideshow that could detract from the wedding itself.

But something even worse had happened. The banquet supplies had run out before the party was over. This could result in an irreparable blow to Micah's reputation in a small town like Cana. So he began to panic as he noticed a decline in the quality of the grape juice being served. You see, the right way to cater drinks was to put out the best stuff first, and then when people were a bit tired of feasting and could no longer tell the difference, to bring out the inferior drink. That strategy saved lots of money, much of which went into Micah's pockets. But when the quality declined, the quantity was starting to run low.

That's when the strangest thing of all happened. Just as supplies were running out, a servant brought Micah a cup of juice to check out. It was the sweetest, freshest juice he had ever tasted! And there was

What was the best (or the worst) experience you ever had at someone else's wedding?

plenty to go around! Now he *knew* these people were strange. Saving the best for the end of the feast just didn't make sense! Everybody knew that wasn't the way things were supposed to go! Micah hoped that this wasn't going to set any precedents for the future.

One last strange thing. Micah didn't remember ordering this particular brand of juice. . . .

 Bible Search
(John 2:1-11)

John 2 opens with a simple story about a wedding where the beverage runs out before the end of the feast. Jesus shows up and rescues a young couple and their caterer from embarrassment. But is that all there is to this story, or is something deeper going on?

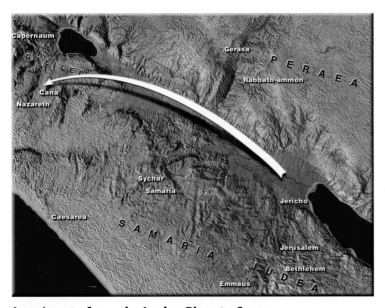

Jesus' route from the Jordan River to Cana

In the first lesson, we became aware of the absence of parables in the Gospel of John. Since parables were a major method in Jesus' teaching, their absence in this Gospel is remarkable. But we will discover in this unit that their role in the Gospel is replaced by the stories about Jesus and His miracles. Beneath the surface of each historical account is a deeper meaning that teaches us something special about Jesus. As the first miracle in the Gospel, the wedding-at-Cana story is the first of these living parables.

Answer the following questions on the basis of the biblical text:

1. When did the wedding take place? John 2:1.
2. Who seems to have had a special concern about the arrangements related to the wedding? John 2:2, 3.
3. In John's Gospel, what did Jesus mean when He said that His "time has not yet come"? John 2:4; 7:25, 30; 8:20.
4. What were the stone water pots normally used for? John 2:6.
5. What was the master of the banquet's (the caterer) assessment of the quality of the wine Jesus had produced? John 2:10.
6. How many miracles had Jesus done before this occasion? John 2:11.
7. How did Jesus reveal His glory in the Gospel of John? John 2:11; 12:23-25, 32, 33.

Important concepts lie just below the surface of this brief Bible study. Changing water into wine symbolized something bigger than a mere physical miracle. The water was not just any water; it was water set aside by the Jews for ceremonial washings. The wine was not just any wine; it was "the best."

John uses this story as a gentle criticism of legalism and formalism. God had originally given the Jews many instructions regarding washings and cleansings, intended to represent their need for cleansing from sin. But the religious people of Jesus' day were obsessed with washing rituals, among other things (see also Matthew 15:1, 2). Washing is good. It is sanitary. As a religious expression, it can remind us of God's cleansing us from sin. But Jesus replaces the water of ceremonial washings with something better, the tasty juice of the grape, a symbol of His blood.

That brings us to the other point highlighted here. John's portrayal of the story presents a series of indirect references to the Cross. The wedding took place "on the third day," a reference to Jesus' resurrection (see Matthew 16:21; Luke 24:7, 21, 46; Acts 10:40; 1 Corinthians 15:4). Jesus turns water into wine, a symbol of His blood (Luke 22:20; 1 Corinthians 11:25, 26). References to both Jesus' "time" ("hour" in the Greek) and His "glory" are pointers to the Cross. And in the only two times in this Gospel that Jesus is described as speaking to His mother, He calls her "woman": in the wedding story here and at the cross itself (John 19:25-27).

In a special way, therefore, this charming wedding story becomes a parable of the Cross and of the glory of God's character that would be manifested there. These two themes are continued in the following story about Jesus' cleansing of the temple.

Bible Search
(John 2:13-22)

Read John 2:13-22 and answer the following questions:

8. What occasion brought Jesus to Jerusalem?
9. What was going on in the temple courts?
10. How did Jesus respond?
11. When challenged about the authority under which He acted this way, what did Jesus say?
12. What did Jesus mean by "temple"?
13. Does this concept of "temple" apply only to Jesus' body? 1 Corinthians 6:19, 20.

The animals being sold in the temple courts were available for sacrifices, making the "marketplace" a genuine and needed service to long-distance travelers. The money exchanging was necessary because the temple did business only in a unique temple currency.

While other sources suggest that there was a lot of deception and corruption involved in the temple-court sales, that doesn't seem to be the issue here in John. The problem here is that the activity, while meeting a legitimate need, was located in a place that should have been devoted exclusively to teaching, worship, and prayer.

Journaling
(Experience)

Are there areas of your life where good things are "cluttering up" your life or distracting you from the better things? Ask God to help you identify those "good" things that get in the way of a fuller relationship with Jesus. What areas of your "temple" would God like to cleanse at this time? How would He like to go about it?

Good, Better, and Best

In John 2:1-22, we see good things getting in the way of the best. It is no different today. Everyone seeks meaning and a sense of value out of life, but few seek it in Jesus. Instead, people try to find "life" by accumulating things, by performing in ways that bring praise, and by developing relationships with admired people.

Chester thought you could find life in possessions. He grew up in the drug-infested streets of Fort Apache, the South Bronx. In his neighborhood, young people often admired pimps and prostitutes because they drove expensive cars and wore fancy clothes. When I asked Chester what he thought happiness was, he said, "Happiness is a big, black Cadillac!" Similarly, bumper stickers proclaim things like "He who dies with the most toys, wins!" and "The only difference between the men and the boys is the price of their toys."

Unlike Chester, I am more susceptible to the performance trap. If I perform well and others praise me for it, I feel more valuable as a person. This came home to me the day I made four errors at third base in a slow-pitch softball game. I was depressed for three days afterward! How stupid! Yet how real! Many people would give almost anything to be a sports hero or a movie star, to be considered the best in the world at what they do.

People also seek life in terms of "who you know." If you have a good relationship with the richest, the brightest, the smartest, the most famous, and/or the most powerful people in your world, you feel more valuable as a human being. Adultery often happens, not because someone is prettier or nicer than a person's spouse, but out of the need to be affirmed and held valuable by someone else.

If true life were found in possessions, performance, and people, professional athletes would be the happiest people on earth.

Possessions, performance, and people are good things. They are part of the spice of life, but they are not life itself. If true life were found in possessions, performance, and people, professional athletes would be the happiest people on earth. After all, many of them make millions of dollars a year, they are admired by people all over the world, and they have all the romantic options anyone could possibly want. Why, then, is drug abuse a major issue in their lives? Why are some players angry and dysfunctional? Because life, real life, cannot be found in money, performance, and people alone.

No matter how many possessions you may have, they are never enough. And those you have rust, rot, break, crash, or get hopelessly scratched up. Athletes get old and frail, beauty queens get old and wrinkled, and teachers get old and forgetful. Loved ones sometimes leave you, disrespect you, divorce you, and/or die when you are least prepared for it. Life is frightfully insecure if based on such good things as possessions, performance, and relationships with other people.

But life is not without hope. If we could find a friend who knows all about us, yet loves us just the way we are (so we know he will not change his opinion of us), who is genuinely valuable (a superstar), and who lives forever (so we won't be bereaved by death), we could have a strong sense of self-worth and meaning in our lives. And that sense of self-worth wouldn't be hostage to the ups and downs of the stock market, the highs and lows of our daily performance, or the moods and whims of our friends and relatives.

I have good news for you. Such a friend lives. His name is Jesus. He is worth the whole universe, yet He knows all about us and loves us as we are. And He will never die, so we can know that we have security in Him throughout eternity. To have Jesus is to have life, even in poverty, sickness, and bereavement. To know Jesus the way John knew Jesus is to understand why the martyrs chose to die rather than reject Him. They discovered that life without Jesus just wasn't worth living.

 Journaling
(Experience)

What do I do when I'm feeling down about my life? Do I turn naturally to Jesus, or do I seek comfort in eating, shopping, talking on the phone, getting a task done,

and/or competing harder at games?

 Journaling
(Prayer)

Write a prayer committing your possessions, your performance challenges, and all of your relationships to Jesus. Be as specific as possible (CDs, clothing, test preparation, best friend, etc.). Invite Him to provide the sense of meaning and self-worth that you have previously sought from other sources.

Foretastes of the Cross

At the conclusion of the first part of the Bible study, we noticed a number of concepts embedded in the basic wedding story that acted as "foretastes" of the Cross (third day, woman, time, wine, glory). This theme continues in the cleansing-of-the-temple episode. When challenged by what authority He had cleansed the temple, Jesus alluded to His divinity by referring to His body as a temple. Thus when Jesus said, "Destroy this temple, and I will raise it again in three days," He was clearly referring to His death on the cross and the resurrection that would follow.

It is the Cross that establishes the value of a person. When the Creator of the universe (more valuable than everything in the universe, including all the toys we often worship, and everyone in it, including all the great athletes and movie stars whom people often worship) decides to die for you and me, it places an infinite value on our lives. The depth of Jesus' sacrifice is a statement about the value of every person. If I am that valuable to the greatest person in the universe, then it doesn't matter whether I'm rich or poor, great or small, famous or ordinary; and it doesn't matter what anyone else thinks of me. I am truly valuable in Christ. And the Cross is the place where that value is demonstrated without question.

No wonder Paul said, "May I never boast except in the cross of our Lord Jesus Christ, through which the world has been crucified to me, and I to the world" (Galatians 6:14). Paul could turn his back on the allurements of the world, its possessions, performance, and people, because he had found meaning and value in something far more stable and satisfying, the Cross of Jesus Christ. That

Reaction

34

Discussion Questions

1. Why would Jesus take time to attend a wedding when His mission was to save the whole world? What role did His attendance at the wedding play in His overall mission?

2. At what point in the wedding story does it become clear that this is not simply a charming story about a wedding? Why?

3. If you were allowed to choose one miracle to jump-start a new ministry for God, what miracle do you think would have a significant impact on people in today's world? Why?

4. When is it appropriate to be angry about things that are going on in the church? In the lives of family and friends? Is there spiritual danger in exercising "righteous indignation?"

5. Does Jesus' example in this story permit us to use violence against wrongdoing at times? How do you think Jesus would respond if He came upon a bank robbery in progress? A woman being raped? A racially motivated riot? A rock concert or a bingo game in church?

6. How is it that useful practices, such as providing sacrifices for travelers, deteriorate into rackets? Why is it that religious practices tend to outlive their usefulness?

Expanded Horizons

1. Compare the temple-cleansing scene in John with those of Matthew, Mark, and Luke. What are the major similarities and differences? What is the main concern of Jesus in each of the accounts of Matthew 21:12-17; Mark 11:15-19; and Luke 19:45-48? Write your answer as a short essay.

2. In a paragraph describe Jesus' relationship with His mother based on John 2:3-5 and 19:25-27. Then read Matthew 13:53-58 and Mark 3:20, 21, 31-35. How do these passages affect your assessment of the

same Cross is a central theme of the Gospel of John.

Journaling
(Insight)

How has the Cross become clearer to you personally because of your study of this Gospel thus far? In your own words, express

the relationship between the Cross and the things we strive for every day.

Anchor Text

"To those who sold doves he said, 'Get these things out of here! How dare you turn my Father's house into a market!' " (John 2:16).

relationship? Write a paragraph developing your further understanding.

3. Use the marginal references in

your Bible to find the psalm quoted in John 2:17. List all the items of similarity between the two passages.

CREATIVE PROJECTS

1. Use the worksheet provided by your teacher to compare the seven major miracles in the Gospel of John with the plagues poured out on Egypt.

2. On the worksheet provided by your teacher, compare the seven major miracles in the Gospel of John with the miracles in the story of Elisha (2 Kings 2 through 9 and 13).

3. Read the *Seventh-day Adventist Bible Dictionary* article on Herod's Temple, describing its construction and its architectural layout. Note especially the illustrations. Then, using materials of your own choosing, create a model of what the temple and its courtyard may have looked like.

Nothing we have ever done or could ever do will stop Him from loving us.

Lesson 4

Grace Is All-inclusive

Lesson Setting

Scripture: John 2:23–4:42.

The cleansing of the temple must have made a deep impression on Nicodemus—he goes to meet Jesus that same night. After spending some time by the Jordan, near the Baptist, Jesus sets out for Galilee, passing through Samaria on the way. There, in the village of Sychar, Jesus encounters a woman in an unforgettable way.

O *h no!* Judith (we don't really know her name) may have thought as she approached the well with an empty jug on her head. *A Jew, of all people!*

The Jew was sitting near her destination, tired, dirty, and all alone. *Won't I ever get any peace?* she groaned to herself.

She already knew the answer to that question. No, she would never have any peace in life. Not only was she a Samaritan, part of a small, despised minority, she was also a defiled and hopeless sinner. Five different men had been attracted by her sensual ways, married her, and then discarded her like a used toy.

She thought for a minute about the lazy lout back home who shared her bed and her dinner table but could never earn her respect. She had enough self-respect not to marry a loser like that. Yet she couldn't bring herself to kick him out of the house. What did that make her? A loser among losers? A loser, that's what she was, a loser attracting other losers. Hopeless.

That's why she was approaching the well at high noon, sweating in the heat of the day. In the morning and evening there would be lots of women at the well. Lots of talk. Lots of laughter. Great gossip. But then the stony silence when she showed up. Everyone looking the other way. Some spitting on the ground near her feet, once or twice even in her face. They despised her loose ways. They hated her for the marriages she had ruined, the husbands she had stolen, the threat to their homes that she remained. No, she didn't need any more rejection. She had learned to come to the well at times when no one else was there.

And now this Jew was sitting there. No way to avoid him. *What's the matter with those Jews anyway?* she thought. *They and*

Have you ever met a person who seemed able to see right through you, almost reading your thoughts? How did that make you feel?

*their silly little temple (well, I suppose it isn't little) back in Jerusalem. Don't they know that Shechem[1] is the real holy city? Don't they know their sacred writings? Don't they know that Abraham built his first altar here?[2] Don't they know that Abraham sacrificed his son Isaac on Mount Gerizim here?[3] That Jacob settled here when he returned from Mesopotamia and built this well?[4] Don't they know that the Israelites had their first worship service here and not in Jerusalem?[5] Don't they know that Jerusalem remained in pagan hands for nearly a thousand years after Abraham? We are the **real** people of God, not them. Boy am I glad I'm not a Jew. Then I'd **really** be a loser.*

Her thoughts became jumbled, and she decided to act as if the Jewish stranger were not there. Maybe she could just slip up to the well, fill her jug, and make a quick get-away before he said anything. No Jew would want to talk to her anyway. It would probably work.

As quietly as possible, she let down the bucket, heard the distant sound of splashing water, and filled her jug. She raised the jug to her head and turned to leave. His voice broke through the turmoil in her mind. "Will you give me a drink?". . .

Bible Search

Jesus Knows

Read John 2:23-25 and answer the following questions:

1. On what grounds did many people at the Passover Feast come to believe in Jesus?
2. How did Jesus respond to their belief?
3. What was the basis for Jesus' response?

Terms like *faith* and *believing* can be used in more than one way in the Gospel of John. Faith, on the one hand, can refer to the saving faith in Jesus that the disciples gained after He turned the water into wine at Cana (John 2:11). The same disciples

38

1. The ancient name of Sychar, where Jacob's well was located.
2. Genesis 12:6, 7.
3. A Samaritan tradition not confirmed in our Hebrew Old Testament.
4. Genesis 33:18-20.
5. Deuteronomy 11:29-32; 27:1-13.

attained an even deeper and more lasting faith after the Cross (John 2:22) and the outpouring of the Holy Spirit (John 7:39). But another type of faith is mentioned in John 2:23-25 and other places: partial faith that is based upon miracles but does not result in a saving relationship with Jesus. In John 2: 23-25 Jesus sees right through some followers' profession of faith and discerns the real motives inside.

People sometimes think that if they could see miracles, they would have more faith. But miracles are no cure for superficial faith; they can even get in the way of true faith, hindering us from perceiving the deeper aspects of a relationship with Jesus.

There is nothing we have done or could do that would cause Him to stop loving us; He already knows all about us.

While we may at first tremble at the knowledge of how deeply Jesus knows everything about us, there is a bright side to consider. If He knows all about us, He knows how to build up our faith. He can impress us in our devotions with the insights we need in order to move deeper into relationship with Him. And His absolute knowledge of our deepest thoughts provides security for our walk with Him. Although He knows all about us, He still accepts us. There is noth-

ing we have done or could do that would cause Him to stop loving us; He already knows all about us. When we confess our sins to Him, we are simply telling the truth about ourselves, something He already knows. We don't need to be afraid, because there is nothing to hide. Because things are already out in the open with Him, there is no danger in being honest. We are freed to become ourselves.

There is freedom and joy in a relationship with someone who knows all about us and loves us just the same. That is the kind of relationship we can have with Jesus.

Journaling
(Experience)

Invite Jesus to "read your heart" and open up whatever insights about yourself He would like to share. Commit yourself to an hour of complete honesty with God; then write in your journal whatever significant thoughts come to mind.

Journaling
(Prayer)

Ask Jesus to make you more open to His kind yet searching gaze. Thank Him for His complete acceptance of you in spite of all He knows. Thank Him for the freedom that comes with honesty.

Bible Search
He Came by Night

In the Gospel of John, the narratives become living parables of the spiritual realities offered in Jesus. In Nicodemus, we see a living example of a person whose faith was based on miraculous signs. He comes to Jesus late in the evening the same day that Jesus cleansed the temple (John 2:13-22).

Read John 3:1-21 and then answer the following questions:

4. With what word does the Nicodemus narrative begin?

In the original this word indicates that the Nicodemus story continues the theme of the previous passage, John 2:23-25.

5. On what basis does Nicodemus consider Jesus a teacher who has come from God?

When Nicodemus says, "We know,"

it indicates that he speaks for others, that he is a representative figure. In this story Nicodemus represents those in the previous passage who saw what Jesus did in the temple and came to have growing faith as a result.

6. How does Jesus expose the inadequacy of Nicodemus's faith?

This story shows Jesus reading the heart of another human being. He knows! The kingdom of God is not entered by being born into a particular race or nation. It is a matter of personal decision.

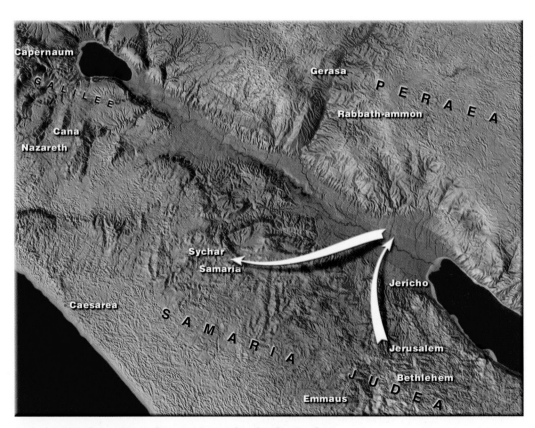

Jesus' route from Jerusalem to Samaria via the Jordan.

7. How can people come to a growing faith?

8. What is the basis for the faith that leads to eternal life?

9. To whom is eternal life made available?

In the Nicodemus story, John continues the themes emphasized in chapter 2. Jesus knows all about Nicodemus, He replaces Nicodemus's religious ideas with a radical new birth, and once again the Cross is the ground for everything that Jesus offers.

Bible Search

She Came by Day

The Nicodemus story is about a man who comes to Jesus at night. In John 4 we have a story about a woman who comes to Jesus at noon. The oppositeness of these details should raise our awareness that there may be a special relationship between these two stories.

Read John 4:1-42 and answer the following questions:

10. Why does Jesus stop at Jacob's well?

11. When Jesus requests a drink from the Samaritan woman, how does she respond?

12. What does Jesus offer her, and what did it represent?

Jesus is clearly on the same subject as He was in John 3.

13. What makes the woman believe that Jesus is a prophet?

14. With what does Jesus replace Samaritan worship on Mount Gerizim? John 4:21-24.

15. Who does she eventually come to believe Jesus is?

16. What happens as a result of the woman's testimony?

17. What do the Samaritans come to believe about Jesus?

In the story of the Samaritan woman, John continues the themes of chapters 2 and 3. Jesus knows all about the Samaritan woman. He reads her heart and her history. And that knowledge gives her the confidence to confess Him. In return, Jesus replaces Samaritan worship with a better faith based on spirit and truth.

Nic and Judith:
The Attraction of Opposites

As we close this lesson, let's note both similarities and differences in these two stories to see where John might have been leading us. Nicodemus is a man; the Samaritan is a woman. He is a Jew, a Pharisee no less; she is a despised Samaritan. He comes by night; she comes at noon. He is rich (John 19:39); she is poor or she wouldn't have been fetching her own water. He is highly educated ("the" teacher of Israel—John 3:10); she is illiterate (a woman in first-century Palestine). He is pious (a Pharisee); she is an adulteress. He is highly respected; she is despised and rejected, even by her own Samaritan neighbors. He has a great name, known from ancient writings outside the Bible; she is anonymous. He lives in the holy city, Jerusalem; she lives in Sychar, which means "drunkenness." He is open to believe, yet slow to accept; she is suspicious at first, yet quick to embrace Jesus when she realizes who He is.

In these two stories we see an acted illustration of John 3:16. God sent His Son so that "whoever believes" might have eternal life. In these two individuals we see the opposite extremes of that "whoever." No matter who you are, no matter what you have done, no matter what your pedigree, no matter how others treat you, Jesus exhibits a glorious lack of prejudice. Whoever wants to may come. There are no conditions of race, religion, sex, custom, wealth, performance, or personal appearance. All are welcome to receive Him. He is truly the "Savior of the World" (John 4:42).

 **Journaling**
(Insight)

In what way(s) have the stories in this

Reaction

Discussion Questions

1. Do you think people sensed immediately that Jesus "saw right through them"? If so, how did that affect their relationship with Him?

2. How can we gain a clearer insight into the deceitfulness of our own hearts? In what type of setting are you most willing to confess your mistakes to others? How can the church help to create such settings?

3. To what degree is it possible for Christians today to have the kind of discernment of others' thoughts, motivations, and feelings that Jesus had?

4. Why do there seem to be so few miracles in the world today? How do miracles become hindrances to true faith? How would secular people respond to the kind of miracles Jesus did?

5. Would you have liked living next door to Nicodemus? Would you have liked having him as elder of your church?

6. Would you consider Nicodemus a timid man or a bold one? Why?

7. Jesus patiently refocused the woman's repeated attempts to change the subject and avoid the confrontation He had initiated. How does one know when to push someone, as Jesus did with Nicodemus, and when to back off, as He did with the woman at the well?

8. What would it have been like to live next door to the Samaritan woman? Would Jesus' acceptance of her increase or decrease your faith in Him? Why?

lesson affected your understanding of Jesus?

 Journaling
(Experience)

To what degree does your treatment of parents, friends, and "enemies" compare with that exhibited by Jesus in the story of the woman at the well?

**Anchor Text**

"For God so loved the world that he gave his one and only Son, that whoever believes in him shall not perish but have eternal life" (John 3:16).

43

Expanded Horizons

1. Compare what we know about Nicodemus from John 3:1-21 with John 7:45-52 and 19:38-42. Based on all three texts, write in two or three paragraphs your total impression of Nicodemus as a person.

2. On the worksheet "Jesus and the Samaritan Woman" provided by your teacher, continue your study regarding the Samaritan woman.

 CREATIVE PROJECTS

In a concordance, look up all the words in the Gospel of John related to *faith* and *believing*. Note in each case whether the word is a noun, a verb, or some other part of speech. Try to group the usages into categories. What did you learn about the role of "believing" or "faith" in the Gospel of John?

God specializes in the impossible.

Lesson 5

The Struggle to Be Real

Lesson Setting
Scripture: John 4:43-54.

The story in this section is one of the most significant in the entire Gospel of John for the devotional life. It portrays a man with doubts and fears who nevertheless approaches Jesus with a request. The story leads us to a deeper understanding of how we can develop faith and authenticity in a world that promotes self-reliance and image.

What a difference a day makes! The sky was bluer, the grass was greener, everyone he passed on the road seemed friendlier; life was suddenly good, very good. But the day had started very differently.

Basilico (we don't know his real name, but *Basilico* means "royal official" in Greek)* woke up in Capernaum that morning to the realization that unless drastic measures were taken, his son would die. The boy had been ill for several weeks, and it was clear that his body systems were in the last stages of a bitter struggle for life.

Basilico loved his son and longed to do something to help. He remembered that a few months before, Jesus had lived in his village and had healed many people. But now Jesus had taken a long trip south.

Would He come back in time? Would He be able to do anything anyway? Was He really a prophet, as people said? What if His miracles were a fraud? What if they were from Satan? Basilico was confused, but he was running out of options.

Just when all seemed lost, word came that Jesus had returned to Galilee and was visiting Cana. Despair turned to hope. Nothing else had worked. Getting Jesus to come to Capernaum seemed worth a try. But Cana was sixteen miles and 2,700 feet of altitude away. That would be a stiff hike in anybody's book. And then he would have to talk Jesus into coming back with Him that same day.

He set out at six in the morning to the sound of his son's gasping breath and hacking cough. There was no time to lose! Driven by hope and desperation, Basilico attained a pace he could never have sustained otherwise. Around noon, he stopped

Have you ever faced the reality that someone close to you was about to die? How did you feel at that time? What role, if any, did God seem to play in that situation?

* The man was a bureaucrat in the government of Galilee, serving under one of the Herods.

briefly to rest, having climbed to within a couple of miles of Cana. He pondered how he ought to approach Jesus when he found Him. It simply would not do for Jesus to know that he had doubts. He must approach Jesus in full confidence that Jesus could heal His son.

Bible Search

Read John 4:46-54 a couple of times and then answer the following questions:

1. What is the setting of this story? John 4:43-45.
2. What kind of job does the leading character hold? What is his problem?
3. Where did both Jesus and the royal official live? John 2:12; 4:46.
4. What did the royal official want Jesus to do?
5. What did Jesus say in response to the first request?
6. To what earlier group in the Gospel was Jesus comparing the Galileans? John 2:13-25.
7. What did Jesus say in response to the second, more desperate request?
8. How did the royal official react to the second statement?
9. At what time was the child healed?

The fact that the servants were sent out and that the men met them the day after the royal official met Jesus indicates that he took his time heading home, stopping somewhere for the night. The word of Jesus brought him to genuine faith, so he did not need to hurry home and find out whether the boy had been healed or not.

10. How can someone develop faith? Romans 10:17.

Journaling
(Experience)

Have you ever prayed for someone who was sick? How did God respond? How did you feel about it? How does it affect your relationship with God when you are sick?

Journaling
(Insight)

What aspects of the royal official's experience can you relate to?

Developing Faith

This delightful story addresses a couple of issues. First is the process by which the royal official was led to genuine faith. It all began in a basic acquaintance with Jesus as fellow citizens in the same small village (John 2:12; 4:46). Then there was a point of need—his son lay dying.

When the royal official heard that Jesus was accessible, he brought his problem to Him. But Jesus' initial response indicates that the man, like Nicodemus before him, was an example of many in whom saving faith is still developing. It seems that the Galileans on the whole welcomed Jesus outwardly but did not really believe in Him (John 4:43-45). They were quick to be awed by miracles and spectacular works, but they were slow to respond to His words. The miracles may actually have become stumbling blocks on the way to a true appreciation of Jesus.

A Galilean himself, the royal official was

46

confronted by the reality of his partial faith. He did not rely on the naked word of Jesus but required physical evidence before he would believe. He was startled to discover that he could not hide his lingering doubts about Jesus. Realizing that he might lose all on account of unbelief, he finally threw himself at the feet of Jesus in desperation. Surely if Jesus could read the secrets of his

Realizing that he might lose all on account of unbelief, he finally threw himself at the feet of Jesus in desperation.

heart (John 2:23-25), He could do whatever He wanted to with the man's request.

Then Jesus speaks the shocking word that He doesn't need to travel to Capernaum; He can heal at a great distance. The word of Jesus is the final piece that brings faith to the royal official. "Faith comes from hearing the message, and the message is heard through the word of Christ" (Romans 10:17). He grasps the word of Christ, and he believes.

But belief brings with it a test. Would he act on that newfound faith? Would he head home, believing that his son will live, or would he continue to beg Jesus to come home and touch? His actions demonstrate his newfound faith. With confidence he turns and heads for home, secure in the

promise of Jesus. If he had hurried downhill, he could have made it back to Capernaum before night. Instead, he takes the scenic route and spends time talking with people along the way. He even stays overnight. He takes so long going home that the family sends the servants to look for him. The servant joyfully announces that the boy was healed, the very hour when Jesus spoke. The man not only starts for home at Jesus' command, he does so in a manner that indicates he has fully accepted Jesus' word. An evidence of faith is action. To go home with assurance yet without Jesus is to believe that His word is as good as His touch.

How can we apply this faith lesson to our lives today? When God knows it is in our best interest to grant a physical blessing to a specific prayer request, this story would suggest four steps in receiving God's gift. (1) **Know that you have a problem**. This is not as simple as it sounds but will be discussed further in the second part of this lesson. (2) **Take your problem to Jesus**. Take it to Him in prayer. Don't be afraid to share it with a prayer partner or a prayer group. (3) **Receive the word that your need has been met**. The words of Jesus to us are found in the Bible. If we want to hear His words, we need to know the Word. That is why Bible study is such an important part of the academy curriculum. You never know which lesson will provide the key to one of life's problems in your future. (4) **Speak and act the idea that God is going to do the right thing**. It is not enough simply to hear the Word. The Word becomes real to us when we *act* on it and when we *tell others* about our faith. Genuine belief results in corresponding confidence that we know God will do the right thing.

But what if we are like the royal official? What if our belief is mixed with unbelief? What if we have doubts? This story suggests that the doubts need to be confronted with words of faith and action. Take God at His word. *Do* what the Bible says—and faith will come. Talk faith—and you will have more faith (see *The Ministry of Healing*, 251-253).

Mrs. Suttoni learned the above steps one Sabbath. Wanting a deeper relationship with Jesus, she decided to spend time every morning receiving His words through the study of the Bible. She made herself the commitment to get up early on Sunday and begin studying the book of Romans with the help of Martin Luther's commentary. She began to act by laying out her Bible and Luther's book at her study desk on Saturday night.

Sunday morning she awoke with a splitting headache, unable to study. She prayed and said, "Lord, I know You want me to spend time with You this morning, so please take the headache away." She waited ten minutes, and nothing happened. She prayed again, and nothing happened. Then she remembered step four, "Speak and act God's answer." So she told God, "I know You want me to spend time with You, so I will do my best; the headache is Your problem." She began to study, headache and all. About ten minutes later, it dawned on her that the headache was gone. That incident had a giant impact on her faith.

 **Journaling**
   (Prayer)

Thank God for the gift of faith in your life. Commit yourself to the steps of faith development.

Steps to Authenticity

The royal official didn't know the depths of his unbelief until confronted directly by Jesus. We, too, are often unaware of our sinfulness and unbelief. We are like Laodicea, the church in Revelation whose self-concept is much different from reality (Revelation 3:17). We face the reality of Jeremiah 17:9: "The heart is deceitful above all things." How can you bring a problem to Jesus when your heart is deceiving you, when you don't even know that you have a problem? **How can you "get real" with God?**

The most effective path to true authenticity before God is a devotional encounter with Him.

1. **Through Bible study** we discover that God works with real people who make mistakes, like David and Peter and Nicodemus. We don't have to be afraid to confess sins and problems to Him— He already knows them. And we find out that He doesn't give up on people who make mistakes. So we gain the courage to get real with God.

2. **Through prayer** we seek to be real with God. This is not always easy. Have you ever lied to God in prayer? "Dear Lord, I love You so much." But in reality, in the back of your mind you are thinking, "Boy, I'd like to punch You right in the nose." Yet God prefers that we tell it like it is in prayer. Jesus cer-

tainly did. "Why have you forsaken me?" If Jesus could be honest with God, it cannot be a sin for us! The Lord wants to hear our deepest needs, our deepest feelings, yes—even our anger. Anything but trying to fool Him with sweet-talking words that mean nothing.

3. **Through journaling** we can bring both our Bible study and our prayers into sharp focus. The writing process draws out depths of self-understanding that often go untapped without it. The writing process can help us develop a deeper understanding of our need for God in specific areas of life. Many of us are gifted with the temperament that knows and uses all the words in every language except the two that express "I'm sorry." We desperately need God's help through study, prayer, and journaling in order to discover the truth about ourselves. But even these three steps may not be enough.

4. **Accountability to others** can enhance our accountability to God. There is no substitute for the checks and balances that come into our life when we become willing to hear the truth about how others see us. Authentic Christians can usually point to specific people who understand and love them yet are willing to tell the truth about the quality of their behavior.

We can develop accountability in a number of ways. We can open ourselves to selected friends who are strong enough and honest enough to tell us how other people see us. We can participate in small groups in which people feel safe in opening themselves up. We can develop prayer partners who will hold us to account in our devotional life. If none of these seem available, we can see a professional counselor, a person trained to help people open up the truth about themselves.

People today are hungry for a faith that is real and that makes a difference in everyday life. We can find such a faith when we open ourselves to God in the context of a community of people who are together on a journey toward God in Jesus Christ. The grace and kindness we find in Jesus through the gospel gives us the courage to face the truth about ourselves. We can also take courage that the same prophet (Jeremiah) who warned us about the deceitfulness of our hearts (Jeremiah 17:9) also promised, "You will seek me and find me when you seek me with all your heart" (Jeremiah 29:13).

 Journaling
(Experience)

What steps toward authenticity make the most sense to you at this stage of your experience? Where do you see God leading you right now?

 Anchor Text

"The heart is deceitful above all things and beyond cure. Who can understand it?" (Jeremiah 17:9).

49

Reaction

Discussion Questions

1. If the royal official was a Gentile, how might that affect the relationship between this story and those of Nicodemus and the Samaritan woman?

2. How does this story illustrate the second-generation theme of the gospel?

3. Why do you think Jesus would say, "A prophet has no honor in his own country," when the Galileans welcomed Jesus gladly (see John 4:43-45)?

4. What kind of impression do you think the royal official would have received living in close proximity to Jesus (ancient Capernaum was only one hundred yards wide)? What groundwork might Jesus have done to prepare the official for faith later on?

5. Why is it so hard to "be real"? Is it easier to be real one-on-one or in a group? Why?

1. A. To what previous event in the first four chapters of the Gospel is John 4:45 referring?
   B. How does John 2:23-25 explain the apparent contradiction between the positive reception the Galileans gave Jesus (John 4:45) and His statement that a prophet has no honor in his own country (John 4:44)?

2. Describe an experience in which you asked God for something, but you didn't get it. List the possible reasons why God didn't answer as you requested.

Forgiveness releases the past and creates a new future.

Lesson 6

Putting the Past Behind You

Lesson Setting

Scripture: John 5:1-47.

Jesus encounters a paralyzed man near a pool on the Sabbath day. Although the man's disease was self-inflicted, Jesus heals him and gets in trouble for it. In response to His critics, Jesus roots His healing powers in His position as the Giver of Life.

What is life anyway? How would I know; I never had one! All I do is lie around waiting for something to happen, but it never does—at least not for me. I have no friends. . . . I guess I never had any friends—at least not since **this** happened to me. I have no money. I can't work. I'm bored. And I know in my heart that nothing will ever change. Why am I here?

The crippled man lay on a mat beside a pool in Jerusalem. Rumor had it that every so often an angel came down and disturbed the waters of the pool. The first one into the pool after the water was disturbed would be cured of whatever disease he or she had. Huge crowds came to be healed, so much so that the man often couldn't even see the pool from where he lay. The least trembling of the water resulted in such a stampede that some people had been trampled to death in the process. For years now he had watched the water, waiting for a chance to be healed; but whenever the water was troubled, someone else would be in first. It was hopeless. As the years went by, the man's eyes glazed over in despair. Paralysis of body became paralysis of mind.

While time dragged on, the man sometimes allowed himself a few moments of regret. As a young man he had engaged in some very risky behaviors, "sin" the rabbis called it. They had warned him that sin would lead to sickness and death, and in his case it had—a living death! What was it that drove him to sin even when he had tried to stop? What kind of emptiness had pushed him to continue in destructive behaviors? Had he known the consequences of his sins, would he have quit in time? Or was he just doomed to this kind of existence? Thirty-eight years of suffering!

Describe a time when you felt stuck in a situation, with seemingly no chance to escape. What does hopelessness feel like? What kind of body language and facial expression best represent hopelessness?

Did he really deserve this?

But even worse than the paralysis was the rejection. Because his sickness was the consequence of his sinful actions, most people, especially the religious, had rejected him. Abandoned to his fate and alone with his thoughts, he found that depression came easily.

Suddenly, a kind face bent over him and broke through his glazed stare. He saw in that face the compassion of a Man who knew what it was like to suffer rejection. He saw interest and concern. The Man said, "Do you want to get well?"

What kind of question is that? the crippled man thought, *Do I want to get well? Does a pig like mud? Does a Roman want power? Do I want to get well? Who is this Man, anyway?*

 Journaling
(Insight)

How does the knowledge that Jesus experienced rejection affect my own memories of rejection?

 Journaling
(Experience)

The question Jesus asked the man was, "Do you want to get well?" What area of my life right now would lead me to say to Jesus, "I want to get well"?

 Bible Search

Read John 5 through and then answer the following questions:

1. Describe the location and the design of the Pool of Bethesda.

    The name *Bethesda* meant "House of Mercy," but little mercy was shown to the hundreds who sought healing there. In this story Jesus shows mercy at the place where people looked for mercy.

2. How long had the man in this story been an invalid?

    Although the King James Bible states that an angel of the Lord stirred up the healing waters, the better biblical manuscripts leave out that element of the story (see the explanation in *The Desire of Ages*, 201). It would have been strange for God to arrange a healing mechanism where the least sick are favored over the truly needy.

3. What words did Jesus speak to the invalid?

    One sentence from Jesus overcame thirty-eight years of paralysis.

4. Did the man respond in some way before he was cured?

5. What day was this?

6. When the man was reprimanded by "the Jews" for carrying his mat on the Sabbath, what excuse did he give?

7. Did the man know who Jesus was?

8. What was the cause of the man's illness?

9. How did Jesus justify healing on the Sabbath?

10. How did Jesus describe what happens when a person believes in Him?

    "Life" in John 5 is more than a physical reality; it is psychological and spiritual as well. Jesus cares for the whole person.

Journaling
(Insight)

What would it mean for Jesus to apply the "power of resurrection" to the biggest problem in my life right now?

 Journaling
(Prayer)

Fill me with the power of Your resurrection, Lord, so I can . . .

 Journaling
(Experience)

Are there any "sins of the mind" in my experience right now?

Implications of the Story

Once again we discover that the stories in the Gospel of John serve as acted illustrations of who Jesus is and what He is like. Several aspects of this story cry out for attention. First of all, Jesus healed the man arbitrarily. He picked one man out of a whole crowd of people—a man who hadn't sought Jesus out, a man who didn't even know Him, a man who expressed no faith in Him before being healed. This reminds me of so many people who have told me that at a decisive point in their lives, they felt God's hand in ways they had not asked for and did not deserve. God does things like this, not to excuse sin, but so we can experience His grace and thereby take courage to deal with sin from then on.

A second startling aspect to the story is that Jesus chose to heal the man on the Sabbath. The rabbis allowed for special acts on the Sabbath in emergencies, but this was no emergency. After all, the man had been crippled for thirty-eight years; surely a day's delay for the sake of the Sabbath would not have made a major difference. Jesus was deliberately making a point here. "It is lawful to do good on the Sabbath day," Jesus had said in Matthew 12:12. What was said there is acted here. The Sabbath is a day when "healing" activity for good is particularly appropriate. When we do good on the Sabbath, we are reflecting the actions God does on that day.

Most interesting of all, however, is the implication of verse 14. When Jesus told the man to "stop sinning," He implied, first of all, that the man's illness was caused by sin in some sense. Continued sin might result in a relapse of the paralysis. But there is an even deeper element here. The form of the word translated "sinning" is extremely continuous. This implies that the man had somehow been continuing in sin, even in a paralyzed state. What kind of sin was Jesus talking about? A paralyzed man cannot rob banks, commit adultery, or kill anyone. Jesus must have been referring to sin of the mind. Apparently, the man's illness was a *psychosomatic one* (physical illness caused by unhealthy mental processes). The physical healing of the invalid was only the tip of the iceberg. Jesus was interested in healing the whole person.

The hurts of the past include not only physical injuries, but emotional, spiritual, and psychological wounds. All these can and need to be addressed by our relationship with Jesus. All other things being equal, a genuine walk with Jesus brightens the facial expressions, soothes emotion, warms the heart, and brings new energy to us physically. This is why Seventh-day Adventist Christianity emphasizes diet, exercise, and attitude. Genuine faith involves every part of life: mental, physical, and emotional, as well as spiritual.

Healing the Hurts of the Past

Having said this, most Christians readily acknowledge that their inner life, particularly the emotional aspect, remains quite unstable even after conversion. The "old nature" rises up again and again to trouble and to torment. Christians, as well as others, have to struggle with unhappy memories, flashes of anger, and unmentionable thoughts. Jesus cares at least as much about the inner life as He does about the outward circumstances.

> **Christians, as well as others, have to struggle with unhappy memories, flashes of anger, and unmentionable thoughts.**

Unwelcome thoughts and emotions can revolve around two types of past events, things we have done and things that have been done to us. Wrongs we have done cause feelings of remorse, regret, and failure. Memories of failure can cause us to become timid and cautious ("I never do anything right") or reckless ("it doesn't matter what I do"). Things others have done to us can cause feelings of anger, grief, and deep resentment.

All of the above emotions came together

as a result of a deep emotional wound that I experienced as a teen. When I was in academy, my hero was one of my teachers. I wanted above all else to be like him when I grew up. As a senior I was the quarterback on the best flagball team in the school. I also had the dubious privilege of refereeing games in which I was not playing.

One day I refereed a game in which this teacher had a rooting interest. Things turned sour almost from the first snap from center.

"That was a stupid call. What's the matter? Are you blind or something? How much is the other team paying you?" Similar comments shouted from the sideline continued for nearly an hour. I bravely acted as if I didn't hear and continued doing my best.

Finally, I followed a power sweep that ended up at the feet of the teacher along the sideline. I was on top of the play and made the call as I saw it. His response was immediate. "I can't believe that call! You are ridiculous! I have never seen such a sorry display of refereeing in all my life!" Struggling to control my emotions, I picked up the football and walked over to the teacher. With a trembling voice, I said, "I'm sorry. I'm doing the best I can." He looked me in the eye and said with contempt, "Your best isn't good enough."

I threw the finest spiral in all my years as

a quarterback; it landed on the roof of a four-story building near the playing field. Then I walked off the field. I found a remote, dark corner and cried for two hours. For months I waited to hear an apology but never received one. Years later I still find it difficult to tell this story without tears.

Why did I cry? Because when my personal hero told me that my best wasn't good enough, I was devastated. I believed that my best would *never* be good enough. I felt that I could not trust those I cared about the most. The future looked dark and meaningless. Thankfully, as the years have gone by, I have learned some practical steps by which people can open themselves up to the healing power of Jesus in even the emotional areas of their lives. I have begun to learn how to deal with painful memories and deep resentments. I have learned that forgiveness is the only way to put the past behind me and move on.

Virtually everyone has had an experience like the one I had on the flagball field. Some may have had a long string of similar experiences. What do you do when your hero crumbles? What do you do when someone you admire lets you down or, even worse, turns on you? The crucial issue in emotional healing is the **how**. How can you overcome painful memories and emotional wounds? In cases where there has been serious abuse, or a record of extreme violence and/or promiscuity, the process of emotional healing is usually long and complex. But there are some strategies that can help along the road to recovery:

1. **Choose healing.** Many people prefer being right to being healed; they wallow in the belief that someone else is to blame for their troubles. They would rather be bitter and vindictive than to pursue the healing that can come only from forgiveness. When hurt or offended, individuals face two choices: get bitter or get better. People sometimes have to "hit bottom," rejecting family or religion or watch their lives spiral into disasters like addiction before they are willing to seek healing change. People rarely recover from emotional pain until they want recovery more than anything else.

2. **Look the past in the eye.** Face the reality about the things you have done or that have been done to you. Seek authentic knowledge about the past. Through prayer, Bible study, journaling, and accountability, seek to sort out reality from the swirl of thoughts and emotions related to that reality (see Lesson 5). Accept responsibility for the choices you have made. Acknowledge the pain that comes from things over which you have no control, such as a negative attitude or unfair treatment from someone whom you trust or admire. Where emotional pain is connected with things that you have done to yourself or to others (sin), true knowledge of the past can lead to confession and repentance. Confession is simply telling the truth about ourselves. When combined with Strategy 9 listed below, it can have an incredibly healing effect.

3. **Discover your value in God's eyes.** It

requires tremendous strength of character to look the past in the eye. This is rarely possible outside a relationship in which you know that you are fully accepted no matter what. The gospel teaches us that the most valuable Person in the universe knows all about us yet loves us with unconditional love. God accepts us as we are. Our value to God is demonstrated at the Cross. We are worth the infinite life of the precious Son of God. And because Jesus will never die again, we can know that He will never abandon us. When we grasp the value we have in God's eyes, the groundwork is laid to give us courage to face the past and deal with it.

4. **Seek support and guidance.** Looking the past in the eye is easier with human support. Finding friends you can trust (these may often be teachers and parents) is a crucial part of the recovery process. For many, especially those who have been traumatized the most, this process may need to begin with a professional counselor, someone who is trained to create a safe environment where people can talk about the things that trouble them the most. Small groups can be an excellent source of caring friends with listening ears.

5. **Invite Jesus into your traumatic memories.** An excellent way to heal traumatic memory is to invite Jesus into the scene. In your journal or imagination, consider how Jesus was affected by the event. What would He say to each person in the scene? How does He feel about what happened to you? About the person you hurt or the person who hurt you? Recreate the memory to include Jesus healing the situation. Make any restitution that He might direct. Accept His forgiveness as needed.

6. **Recognize that we live in a sinful world.** One unfortunate reality of living in this sinful world is that all human beings, even our heroes and friends, are flawed and imperfect. Simply put, sooner or later all of us have to swallow the bitter pill of rejection or disillusionment. You just can't go through life without dealing with disappointments that sometimes can be extremely painful. And it can be especially demoralizing when the person who lets us down is someone in our home, in the church, or at a Christian school. After all, Christians are not supposed to act this way. But with a bit more maturity, we begin to recognize that Christians are all still under construction.

7. **Beware of wallowing in your painful past.** Psychologists have discovered that telling a story over and over again can actually alter one's memory of the event itself. After a while one's perception of the event can replace, in one's memory, what actually happened. Be open to new perspectives about what happened. Sometimes discovering why a person acted as he or she did can help dissolve the pain. Steve, an academy senior, had been offended by the sharp, critical response of one of his teachers. Yet he

chose not to dwell on the incident when he remembered that the man's wife had suddenly died just a few weeks before.

8. **Forgive those who have hurt you.** To forgive someone else is sometimes a blessing to that person, but it is always a blessing to us. Forgiveness is a choice. We may have to choose to forgive several times before we feel that it is changing things very much. To forgive is to break the chains of the past and create a new future. To refuse to forgive is to be filled with resentment, hatred, and anger, which destroy us far more than they hurt the other person. To forgive is to find healing. That is why Jesus longs to help us forgive.

9. **Forgive yourself.** This is usually harder than forgiving others. Forgive yourself for all the times that you have hurt other people out of your own emotional pain. Rather than recounting a litany of the failures of others, it is wiser to humbly reflect upon one's own mistakes. Becoming more discerning of our own callousness and unfair treatment of others may restore perspective to our injured and sometimes self-pity lives. But the good news is that Jesus longs to help us forgive ourselves.

10. **Recognize that everyone has a breaking point.** Sometimes competitive sports, among many other things, can create dynamics that sweep people beyond the point of good judgment. Winning the game can easily become more important than demonstrating

kindness and consideration for the feelings of others. When we lack good sportsmanship, unfortunate incidents take place that linger long past the end of the game. Now that I am a teacher myself, I have found that it is vitally important for me not to let momentary impatience, that I will later regret, erupt into words and actions when dealing with students.

11. **Build new, positive memories.** The day will come when the scar is still there but the pain is gone. We will remember, but it won't hurt anymore. As old memories are healing, it is time to create new, positive images. Remind yourself how valuable you are in Christ. Practice affirming and encouraging others. Use your story to sensitize you to the needs of other hurting people and begin to make a positive difference in their lives. Your journey of personal growth can lead to greater personal authenticity. By memorizing scripture, by practicing the processes and strategies described in these lessons, you can work through the inevitable injustices and disappointments of life. Putting the past behind you is part of the lifelong process called sanctification.

12. **God works in spite of human failure.** In spite of that one teacher's hurtful behavior, God's grace has been more than sufficient. And today I myself am a religion teacher! Isn't it amazing how God works? There have been so many young people and other adults who showed me that God accepts me, even

when my best hasn't been good enough!

Journaling
(Prayer)

Thanks for the Cross; help me to always value myself as You have valued me.

Journaling
(Experience)

What friends and family are You providing for my support? How would You like them to be involved in my life right now? How should I approach them about my needs and problems?

Reaction

Discussion Questions

1. Do you think people were actually healed at Bethesda, or was its reputation based on wishful thinking? Why? Do you think God could participate in healings at such a place? How and why?

2. Why do you suppose Jesus chose such an unpromising situation to make a point about appropriate conduct on the Sabbath? Does His action justify acting as a nurse or doctor on the Sabbath? Would He consider it appropriate to function as a policeman on the Sabbath? A governor or president? A Bible scholar?

3. What does it tell us about sin that a paralyzed man's thoughts could be so characterized?

4. Why do many Christians believe that accepting Jesus should put an end to all emotional difficulties? Why might they think that?

5. Why do most people find it so hard to forgive?

6. What do you think Jesus would say to the victim of rape or abuse? What would He say to the perpetrator?

 **Journaling**

(Experience)

Whom am I having difficulty forgiving? How would You want me to approach them? Whom should I approach first?

 **Anchor Text**

"Later Jesus found him at the temple and said to him, 'See, you are well again. Stop sinning, or something worse may happen to you' " (John 5:14).

Expanded Horizons

1. On one piece of paper, make a list of people you have had trouble forgiving. Decide which person on the list should be your top priority for reconciliation. On a second piece of paper, brainstorm how you would approach that person in order to bring about forgiveness and reconciliation.

2. Using the NIV Bible translation, fill in the blanks on the worksheet provided by your teacher. Note the parallels between John 5:24, 25 and John 5:28, 29. On a separate sheet of paper answer the following:
   A. Which of the passages refers to realities in Jesus' day, and which points to the future end time?
   B. List the words and phrases that justify your conclusion.
   C. Write a paragraph outlining some practical implications of judgment and eternal life being seen as already present.

 CREATIVE PROJECTS

With the help of a concordance list all the words for *judgment* or *judging* in the Gospel of John. Look up and record each of the passages in which the words *judgment* or *judging* are found. Separate those statements that put judging into the future from those that speak of it as present in Jesus' day. Which kind of statement is present in larger numbers, present or future judgment? In a paragraph or two, describe the implications you find in the results of your research.

Jesus makes great endings out of small beginnings.

Lesson 7

Finding the Sacred in the Common

Lesson Setting

Scripture: John 6:1-71.

The author of the Gospel uses the story of feeding the five thousand as a living parable of the spiritual feeding we receive when we enter into relationship with Jesus. When we experience a lack of food, we are hungry. That hunger leads to a longing that enhances the flavor of any food. So the absence of Jesus in our lives leads to restlessness and longing that cannot be filled in any other way.

The disciples and Jesus were exhausted after many weeks of ministry. People needed counseling, physical healing, and sometimes just someone to talk to. Crowds of people. A never-ending stream. While Jesus was the focus of most of the work, the disciples were busy too. They organized the people, screened out frivolous requests, helped where they could, and did their best to protect Jesus from excessive demands.

Finally Jesus called the disciples aside and said, "We need a vacation; let's take off after dark and travel across the lake to that deserted area on the other side." But it was as if they had been set up. When they tried to get into their boat without being noticed, someone raised an alarm. As they cast off from shore, they could hear the sounds of people rushing to the docks to follow them in other boats. When morning came, they discovered that people who didn't own boats had walked around the lake to the other side, converging on them from the north.

Thousands of people were traveling toward Jerusalem for Passover. As they noticed the crowd gathering around Jesus, many asked questions and decided to interrupt their travel for a bit, multiplying the crowd even more. Soon Philip estimated that there were more than ten thousand people trying to get to Jesus (the text says five thousand men plus women and children).

Just as things were getting out of control, Jesus approached Philip. "Philip, with this crowd that includes those who followed after us through the night and travelers who aren't going to make the next rest stop, we have a lot of people who are very hungry. You used to live around here; how do you think we can feed everyone?"

"Are you serious, Master?"

> What is your favorite kind of bread (wheat, white, rye, bagels, etc.)? When Jesus says, "I am the bread of life," what does that mean to you? Can you recall a time when you were really hungry and someone provided a hot, fresh piece of your favorite bread?

"Yes," Jesus said with just a bit of a twinkle in His eye.

"There's no way! We could never find enough food around here. Now what are we going to do?"

Just then Andrew showed up with a little boy whose mom had remembered to pack him a lunch. "Here, Jesus," said the boy. "You can have *my* lunch."

Jesus glanced over the gathering crowd for a minute, then glanced at Philip. The twinkle was still in His eye. With a smile He said, "You know, I think that might be enough. . . ."

Bible Search
(John 6:1-15)

Read John 6:1-15 and then answer the following questions:

1. In what part of Palestine does this story take place?

   The location is unusual in the Gospel of John. In this Gospel Jesus spends most of His time in Jerusalem and the surrounding regions.

2. What event was drawing near at that time?

3. Why was the crowd following Jesus far from their homes on the other side of the lake?

4. What earlier event in Jesus' ministry does the language of John 6:2 recall? John 4:43-45; 2:23-25

   The implication of the statement in John 6:2 is that the great crowd following Jesus on this occasion was made up of superficial believers, people who were impressed by His miracles but who did not have deep and lasting faith in Him.

5. Had time permitted, would the disciples have been able to feed all the people there?

6. What comment did Andrew make to Jesus about the boy's lunch?

7. What happened next?

8. On what other occasion did Jesus handle bread in this way? Matthew 26:26;

Mark 14:22

9. When everyone had finished eating, what command did Jesus give?

10. How did the people react to the miracle, and what was Jesus' response?

 **Journaling**
(Experience)

Describe a time in your life when God

The presence of Jesus cannot be confined to church buildings where the "right" style of worship service is performed.

stretched your meager resources just as Jesus multiplied the boy's lunch in John 6:1-15. In what area of your life could you use a similar miracle today?

Seeing Jesus in the Common

In the Gospel of John, whenever Passover is mentioned, there is always an allusion to either the Lord's Supper or the Cross (or both). John does not include an account of the Lord's Supper in his Gospel, but there is an exquisite theology of the Lord's Supper here in chapter 6. The true meaning of the Passover is to be found in the person of Jesus and in the supper that only He can provide. Once again Jesus takes something that is good (Passover) and transforms it into something even better.

It is interesting, however, that both of John's allusions to the Lord's Supper are found in the context of outdoor lunches, this one on a hillside, the other on a beach (John 21:1-14). In a sense the Communion service, the dinner table, and an outdoor meal share something in common. The presence of Jesus cannot be confined to church buildings where the "right" style of worship service is performed. For those who walk with Jesus, there is a sense in which every meal can become a sacrament, an event in which the real and empowering presence of Jesus is experienced.

You see, were it not for the Cross of Jesus Christ, there would be no bread, no water, no rain, no life. "To the death of Christ we owe even this earthly life. The bread we eat is the purchase of His broken body. The water we drink is bought by His spilled blood. Never one, saint or sinner, eats his daily food, but he is nourished by the body and the blood of Christ. The cross of Calvary is stamped on every loaf. It is reflected in every water spring" (*The Desire of Ages*, 660).

One of the secrets of the devotional life is to learn how to see the presence and the power of Jesus in the common things of everyday life, to sense that He is there with us even though we cannot see, hear, or touch Him. We will return to this concept at the end of this lesson.

 **Journaling**
(Insight)

In what ways would your walk with Jesus be enhanced by a deeper awareness of His presence in everyday activities? How can

65

you make the everyday activities of eating and drinking spiritual events?

 Bible Search

(John 6:22-71)

In John 6:16-21, Jesus and the disciples cross the Sea of Galilee back to Capernaum.

Read John 6:22-71 and then answer the following questions:

11. When they found out that Jesus and His disciples had left the area again, where did the crowd go to look for them?
12. Why did the crowd keep searching for Jesus at this time?
13. What should they have been seeking?
14. How did the ancient Israelites survive in the desert, and what did that have to do with the feeding of the five thousand in this chapter?

A consistent theme in the background of John 6 is the Exodus from Egypt. The feeding of the five thousand recalled the original Passover, when the Israelites escaped from the immediate grasp of the Egyptians. Then the storm episode (John 6:16-21) recalled the perils the Israelites faced at the Red Sea. Now comes a reference to God's guiding of their experience in the desert of Sinai.

15. What is the real "bread from heaven" that God wants to give His people today?
16. What is the spiritual meaning of this "bread from heaven"?
17. Why did the people have a hard time accepting Jesus' claims?
18. In what other way does Jesus express how people enter into relationship with Him and receive eternal life?

19. When people were offended by this last saying, how did Jesus clarify His earlier statements?
20. What was the result of this clarification?

Talking to Deaf Ears

It is clear throughout this chapter that the crowds are relating to Jesus on a material level. They are not searching for spiritual food; they want their physical needs to be satisfied. They want to see more miracles like the feeding of the five thousand. In spite of that awesome event, when the people looked at Jesus, they saw a common everyday human being like themselves, not someone who came down from heaven. They were unable to see the sacred shining through the common. The very physical presence of Jesus became a stumbling block to them. Life is found by accepting the claims that Jesus makes about Himself. Those who believe in Jesus receive all the evidence that they need; they don't need to see miracles in order to believe.

Who is Jesus really? He is much more than just a good man who grew up in Nazareth with Joseph and Mary. No good man would claim to be the Son of God who came down from heaven. To make such a claim, he would either have to be crazy, a deceiver (in neither case would people designate Him a "good man"), or exactly what He claims to be. There is no middle ground—we must either accept Him and all that He stands for or reject Him as insane, or even worse, the perpetrator of the greatest scam of all time. The foolishness of the people in this story is that they insisted on seeing

Jesus as just a good man or even a prophet (John 6:14). These are not really options where Jesus is concerned.

So it is crucial that people recognize exactly who Jesus is. He brings from heaven a revelation of God and about God that is of life-and-death importance to the human race. Eating and drinking the symbols of the "body" and "blood" of Jesus is a graphic way of expressing that only through intimate relationship with Jesus can one have the eternal life that He promises.

The Sacred in the Common

Time and again in the Gospel of John, symbols are drawn from everyday experience, symbols such as bread, water, and light. These symbols help us to connect Jesus' words with things in the context of our everyday lives. No matter how ordinary our lives may be, our relationship with Jesus will deepen and grow as we learn to remember Him in the course of everything we do. As the Bread of Life, Jesus brings us a taste of eternal life, which makes physical food and drink seem insignificant by comparison.

Have you ever been ravenously hungry or thirsty to the point of desperation? Do you remember what it was like to be handed a cool drink or a slice of bread with your favorite spread on it at that time? Jesus wanted memories like that to trigger spiritual meanings, to offer lessons about the life that He came to offer. The message of the Bread of Life sermon is that your need for the spiritual life that Jesus brings is just as desperate as your pangs of hunger and thirst. As the body craves food and drink and sunlight, so the soul craves the presence of Jesus. If Jesus is not received into one's life, human beings will go to all kinds of ridiculous lengths to fill the gap with something else. Inside every human being is a God-sized hole that only Jesus can fill.

What is the secret? It is tying the experience of everyday life with images from the words of Jesus (John 6:63). In Christ all of life can become a sacred encounter, an experience of the presence and power of Jesus Christ in the common affairs of everyday experience. No matter what we do in life, we can recall the words Jesus spoke at the inauguration of the Communion service, "Do this in remembrance of me."

When we sit down at a table to eat, we can remember sunshine, rain, and life. The food production they make possible would all have ceased with sin were it not for the Cross of Jesus. When we lift a glass to drink, we can remember the Water of Life. When we get dressed in the morning, we can think about the robe of Christ's righteousness (His perfect life that offers us as a new perfect record before God). When we relax at home, dry and warm under a sheltering roof, we can recall how the righteousness of Christ shelters us from the ultimate consequences of sin. When we go to sleep at night, we can experience a living parable of human frailty, the end of life. Like Jesus on the cross, we can pray, "Father, into your hands I commit my spirit," knowing we will rise again in the morning, as Jesus did on the first day of the week.

When we attend a wedding, we can think

about the relationship between Christ and the church (Ephesians 5:31, 32). When we get sick, we can think about the one who "took up our infirmities" (Isaiah 53:4). When we suffer, we can recall the one who suffered for us (1 Peter 2:21). And when we come to the end of our lives, we can celebrate that our battle with sin will soon be over. One of the keys to a living relationship with Jesus is to make all the common events of our lives reminders of the words and actions of Jesus.

 **Journaling**
(Experience)
What aspects of your own experience

Reaction

68

Discussion Questions

1. Why do you think Jesus wanted to test Philip by asking where they might buy bread, when He already knew what He was going to do?

2. Why do you suppose that Jesus ordered them to collect the leftover food when He was quite capable of producing as much as needed, whenever needed?

3. What do you consider a proper balance between working and resting? Is it possible to be too dedicated to God's work? How would one know?

4. Why do you think the crowd demanded further signs even after the spectacular event of feeding the 5,000?

5. If someone in your school said that he or she had come down from heaven with a message for you, what would it take to convince you that the person was telling the truth?

6. How do you think Jesus would express the idea to people today that we should eat His flesh and drink His blood?

7. What was it about Jesus' teaching in John 6 that was so hard for the listeners to accept?

could function as symbols or reminders of the words and actions of Jesus?

Journaling

(Prayer)

Invite Jesus to make Himself real in the mundane things of your daily life. Invite Him to provide the evidence of His power and presence that will encourage and strengthen your faith.

Anchor Text

"The Spirit gives life; the flesh counts for nothing. The words I have spoken to you are spirit and they are life" (John 6:63).

69

Expanded Horizons

1. Andrew and Philip both speak to Jesus in this passage. Using a concordance, compare their words here with things they each said and did elsewhere in John's Gospel. In a couple of paragraphs, describe how this helps us understand the response of each of them at the feeding of the five thousand.

2. Compare the account in John 6:16-21 with the accounts in Matthew 14:22-27 and Mark 6:45-52. First, list all the parallels between John and the other two accounts; then list all the points in John's account that differ from the others, including omissions. What unique point do you think John is making? Why?

CREATIVE PROJECTS

With the help of a concordance, study all the passages in all four Gospels that mention Judas Iscariot. Write out a sketch of Judas's character, based on these texts. Compare this with the description by Ellen G. White in *The Desire of Ages*, 716-722. Based on what you've learned about Judas, why do you think he chose to remain with Jesus when many forsook Him as recorded at the end of John 6?

In Christ we have the Presence of the future.

Lesson 8

The Great "I AM"

Lesson Setting

Scripture: John 7:1–8:59.

In this section Jesus travels to the temple in Jerusalem for the Feast of Tabernacles. While there He engages in a series of debates with the crowd and particularly with the Jewish leaders. While this lesson briefly covers the events described in John 7 and 8, the particular focus of this lesson is on the "I AM" statements found in this section and throughout the Gospel. So this lesson is more thematic than textual in approach.

*W*hat did I do to deserve this? wondered Moses as he sat on a rock, surrounded by sheep and the desolate landscape around Mount Sinai. *My life is an endless pattern of unfulfilled potential. A failure without a future, that's me.*

Moses recalled how he had spent his childhood in a slave hut back in Egypt, gradually coming to understand that he had been adopted by the daughter of Pharaoh and would one day be the ruler of all Egypt. At the age of twelve, he moved from the slave hut to the king's palace. There he experienced the finest teachers and the greatest possessions the world had to offer. As he grew older, he was given increasing responsibility in the court. He commanded larger and larger units in the Egyptian army. He was on a fast track to success, power, wealth, fame, and ultimately a revered place of burial in the Valley of the Kings as a new member of the Egyptian pantheon of gods.

But at the very height of his power and success, he remembered the teachings of his birth mother once more. He remembered that he was not really an Egyptian. He was a child of God, a Hebrew, and his real heritage was in the slave huts down in the Nile delta. With one rash act, he threw away his earthly future and identified with an oppressed and helpless people.

And where had it gotten him? Instead of helping them, he himself had lost everything. He had gone from sleeping in a king's palace to sleeping under the stars on stony ground. He had gone from sumptuous banquet tables to scrounging around for whatever one could find in the desert. He had gone from fame to obscurity. He had gone from commanding an army of the fittest and best-trained men in the world to com-

> Describe a time when you met a person who was truly powerful, famous, or awesome in personality. How did you feel and react?

manding a flock of stupid, aimless sheep.

Now he was eighty years old. His life and his opportunities all seemed in the past. The Hebrew people in Egypt were just as much slaves as they had been on the day of his birth. He had accomplished absolutely nothing with his life! With all his mistakes, God must have forsaken him. He remembered the song he had written to God only a few weeks before:

You sweep men away in the sleep of
    death;
they are like the new grass of the
    morning—
though in the morning it springs up new,
    by evening it is dry and withered.

We are consumed by your anger
    and terrified by your indignation.
You have set our iniquities before you,
    our secret sins in the light of your
    presence.

All our days pass away under your wrath;
    we finish our years with a moan.
The length of our days is seventy years—
    or eighty, if we have the strength;
yet their span is but trouble and sorrow,
    for they quickly pass, and we fly away.

Who knows the power of your anger?
    For your wrath is as great as the fear
    that is due you.
Teach us to number our days aright,
    that we may gain a heart of wisdom
                        (Psalm 90:5-12).

O well, thought Moses, *I guess things are about over for me. If God is going to free those Hebrews, He'll have to use someone else.*

Just then Moses noticed a strange thing. A bush over on the mountain was burning. This happened from time to time in the tinder-dry desert of Sinai. But this bush just kept on burning. It didn't burn up! He went over to take a closer look. Suddenly, in the middle of nowhere, he heard a voice calling, "Moses! Moses!"

"I'm right here."

"Take off your shoes, Moses. You're standing on holy ground. I am the God of your fathers."

Moses was terrified and turned his face away from God.

God continued, "I have seen the misery and the oppression My people face every day in Egypt, and I have decided to rescue them and bring them to their own land. So I am sending you to Pharaoh to bring My people out of Egypt."

"Who, me? Why me? Why now? I am nobody and going nowhere. I am too old, and I don't talk very well. Please send somebody else."

"Don't worry, I will be with you. You can do it," God replied.

"But when I get there, who should I tell them sent me?"

"I AM WHO I AM," God replied. . . .

 **Journaling**
    (Experience)

To what degree am I concerned about death? To what degree have I gained peace in the knowledge that Jesus is Lord over death?

72

The Feast of Tabernacles

In John 7:10 Jesus participates in the Feast of Tabernacles at the temple in Jerusalem. His presence at the feast draws Him into repeated confrontations with the religious leadership. These confrontations are recorded in the Gospel of John because they offered the opportunity for Jesus to clarify His mission.

In Palestine there are two basic seasons of the year, an extremely dry summer of four to five months (during which it rarely rains) and a rainy season of equal length spanning the winter. The Feast of Tabernacles comes at that time of year when the summer drought is usually ending (September/October). The winter grains are planted, and the harvest of fruit is celebrated.

Just as God provided water and food to Israel in the wilderness, so He can continue to provide for the needs of the present.

The Feast of Tabernacles commemorated the Exodus and the time of Israel's wandering in the wilderness (Leviticus 23:43), when God provided Israel with water and light (Exodus 13:21, 22; 17:1-7). So two major themes of the feast were water (a water ceremony was a major feature of each day's festivities) and light (torchlight processions were held at night). People lived outside in booths made from palm branches, reminding them of God's watchcare in the wilderness. This reminder of the Exodus taught them that just as God provided water and food to Israel in the wilderness, so He can continue to provide

for the needs of the present.

Bible Search

Jesus as the Great "I AM"

Read John 7 and 8 in light of the following summary:

In John 7 Jesus first debates with His brothers about the timing of His visit to Jerusalem (verses 1-9). Then He debates with the Jewish leadership about the validity of His teachings (10-19), His healing at Bethesda on the Sabbath (20-24), and where He came from (25-36). After the Jewish leaders fail to capture Him (40-52) or embarrass Him (7:53–8:11), chapter 8 continues the debates in the temple courts. The issues of the validity of Jesus' teachings and of His origin (8:12-30) are taken up again. The debate then degenerates into name-calling (31-59). Jesus and His opponents accuse each other of being children of the devil and debate what it means to be called children of Abraham. This section concludes with the dramatic statement of Jesus, "I tell you the truth, before Abraham was born, I am!" (8:58).

This concluding assertion points to one of the major features of John 7 and 8, the presence of a number of special "I AM" statements (signaled by the unusual Greek expression *ego eimi*—pronounced "aygo aymee") on the part of Jesus.

Answer the following questions regarding the "I AM" statements of chapter 8:

1. To what does Jesus compare Himself in John 8:12?

Jesus may have had the sun in mind when He used this expression.

2. How important does Jesus consider this "I AM" concept?

The words "the one I claim to be" are supplied by the translators; the original simply says "I AM."

3. What event will convince the people that "I AM"?

Again, the words "the one I claim to be" are supplied by the translators.

4. When Jesus calls Himself "I AM" in 8:58, what is He claiming?

What is clear from John 8 alone is that the "I AM" statements are of vital importance, that they are associated somehow with the Cross of Jesus, and that they indicate that Jesus was in existence long before He came to this earth as a human being. But before we can fully grasp the meaning of the "I AM" statements in John 8, we need to survey their use throughout the Gospel.

Bible Search

The "I AM" Texts in the Gospel of John

This Bible Search illustrates the three types of "I AM" usages that Jesus makes in the Gospel of John.

Answer the following questions on the basis of the texts provided:

5. In what two settings does Jesus use the phrase "I AM" in a purely human and ordinary way (something like, "Hey,

guys, it's me!")? John 4:26; 6:20.

6. What seven things did Jesus say He is? "I AM the . . ." John 6:35; 8:12; 10:7, 11; 11:25, 26; 14:6; 15:1.

These statements illustrate ways in which Jesus' divinity is exercised for the benefit of those who are in relationship with Him.

7. How will the disciples come to believe that Jesus is the "I AM"? John 13:18, 19.

In John 13:19 the word *He* in "I am He" is supplied by the translators.

Jesus sometimes uses "I AM" all by itself (called by scholars of John the "absolute use") to assert His full equality with the God described in the Old Testament.

Journaling
(Insight)

How has my study of the Gospel of John thus far increased my awareness of the greatness of Jesus?

Bible Search

"I AM" in the Old Testament

While one can learn a great deal from a study of the "I AM" statements in the Gospel of John itself, greater clarity arises when these statements are seen in the light of the way they were used by God in Old Testament times.

Answer the following questions on the basis of the texts provided:

8. To what question of Moses does God answer, "I AM WHO I AM," in Exodus 3:14?

9. What does the "I AM" express in Isaiah 43:10, 11?

10. What other characteristic of the "I AM God" is expressed in Isaiah 46:9, 10?

Within the Old Testament, "I AM" functioned as a name for God, expressing His continual availability to meet human needs, His total uniqueness among all claimants to the title of "god," and His ability to foretell the future accurately.

11. What action will convince people that "I am the Lord"? Ezekiel 34:27, 30, 31.

12. What is the predominant tense in Ezekiel 34:20-31—past, present, or future?

13. What role will God Himself play at that time? Ezekiel 34:20-24.

14. What action shows even the nations that "I am the Lord"? Ezekiel 36:23, 24.

15. What is the predominant tense in Ezekiel 36:22-38—past, present, or future?

In the writings of prophets like Ezekiel, the "I AM" expression is used in the context of the mighty works of future salvation that the Lord will accomplish in the age to come. The Old Testament comes to a climax looking forward to some future time when God will do a mighty work for His people and so be recognized for who He is. The God who will act at that time is the same unique and all-knowing God who met Moses at the burning bush.

The Presence of the Future

The most exciting thing about the "I AM" usages in the Gospel of John comes into focus when we see how Jesus was building on the Old Testament picture. From the Old Testament perspective, God would act as a Good Shepherd to feed and care for His people at the great end-time climax of earth's history. But Jesus declares that the future salvation that was promised in the prophets has become a present reality in Him. He *is* the Good Shepherd that was promised in Ezekiel 34 (John 10:11). He *is* the divine figure (John 8:24, 28, 58) who knows the future ahead of time (Isaiah 46:9, 10; John 13:19). What was future in the Old Testament is made present in Christ.

What was future in the Old Testament is made present in Christ.

In Jesus' "I AM" statements, we see an assertion of His divinity. He is the God of the Old Testament, come down to shepherd His people just as He promised through the prophets (John 8:58). Jesus is none other than the Yahweh of the Old Testament. He is fully and truly God in the highest sense, even while walking on earth clothed in human flesh. He has preexisted throughout eternity (John 8:58). Belief in the divinity of Jesus is essential for salvation (John 8:24).

But there is more. In these "I AM" statements is the assertion that the future has become present in Christ. He can deliver the promised glories of the Old Testament future kingdom to those who believe in Him now. To be in relationship with Jesus is to have the abundance of the future kingdom *now* by faith. In a real sense, we are already living in heavenly places in Christ Jesus (Ephesians 2:6). There is nothing out of reach to those in relationship with Jesus. In Christ there are limitless possibilities. The mighty

There is nothing out of reach to those in relationship with Jesus. In Christ there are limitless possibilities.

things that Jesus (God) did in Old Testament times are brought to earth by Him, and, through Him, by the Holy Spirit.

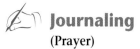 **Journaling**
(Prayer)

Lord, make the heavenly realities of Your kingdom real in my life.

The Truth Sets You Free

We would be remiss if we passed by John 8 and did not reflect for a moment on the awesome comment of Jesus, "You will know the truth, and the truth will set you free" (John 8:32). In the Feast of Tabernacles the two great symbols were water and light. Both of these represent truth, the truth about the person of Jesus ("Come to me and drink," "I am the Light of the world" [John 7:37; 8:12]) and His revelation of the will and character of God (John 3:33, 34; 14:6). For the second generation of Christians, the Jesus focus of the New Testament makes it the greatest revelation of God and of truth

that is available anywhere.

Freedom is one of the greatest needs of human beings. How and in what way does the truth about Jesus set people free?

1. The truth brings freedom from fear. The disciple of Jesus never walks alone, no matter where he or she may go; and in the presence of Jesus, fear is gone, because "perfect love drives out fear" (1 John 4:18). You can walk with confidence when you go on God's errands.

2. The truth brings freedom from self. For most people, the greatest handicap to a fulfilled life is found within themselves. Jesus has the power to change what we cannot change. God takes us beyond where we would naturally be without Him. In Christ, all things become new (2 Corinthians 5:17; Revelation 21:5).

3. The truth also brings freedom from being overly influenced by other people. Many people are paralyzed by fear of what other people may think of them. To know that we are acceptable to God reduces the impact of what other people think or say. We can think and act in terms of what is best rather than being crippled by whether or not others will be pleased with us.

4. The truth brings freedom from sin. Many people have experienced the addictive power of sin. They sin, not because they want to, but because they have to. Sinners don't do what they like; they do what sin likes. Dis-

cipleship with Jesus breaks the chains of sin and empowers people to reach their full potential. "If the Son sets you free, you will be free indeed" (John 8:36).

 Journaling
(Insight)

What difference does this concept of freedom in the gospel make in my life?

 Journaling
(Experience)

To what degree have I experienced the four types of freedom that are available in the gospel? In what circumstances do I find myself concerned about what other people think? In what areas of my life have I experienced the addictive power of sin? What kinds of fears have I experienced in my life recently?

 Journaling
(Prayer)

Lord, help me be willing to allow you to bring your freedom into my life in . . .

Anchor Text

" 'I tell you the truth,' Jesus answered, 'before Abraham was born, I am!' " (John 8:58).

Reaction

1. How do you think Jesus' relationships with members of His family affected His life and ministry? Was the overall effect positive or negative? Why?

2. How do you think the teachers of the law and the Pharisees would have reacted if in the story of John 8:1-11 Jesus had told them to let the woman go? How would they have reacted if He had told them to stone her? What would you have written on the ground if you had been in the place of Jesus?

3. How do you think Jesus' response to the woman taken in adultery should affect the church's response to divorce and remarriage?

4. Do you think Christians or secular people are more likely to misunderstand Jesus today? Explain your answer.

5. Can you think of times in your experience when you or someone else grossly misunderstood the Bible or some theological point? What were the causes of that misunderstanding?

6. What are some things you are proud of in your religious heritage? Do some aspects embarrass you? Why? Is one's religious heritage usually a help or a hindrance in developing a relationship with Jesus? Why?

7. Who do you think had it easier to believe that they were in the presence of God, Moses at the burning bush or the disciples who walked with Jesus every day? Explain your answer.

8. Based on the texts you have studied, do you believe that Jesus *is* the God of the Old Testament or is He *like* the God of the Old Testament? What difference does your answer make?

78

1. List all the issues that divide Jesus and His opponents in John 7 and 8. Is there any progress in the discussion, or do Jesus' opponents keep bringing up the same charges in different words? In a paragraph or two, discuss what we can learn from these texts about handling differences with others today.

2. Read Leviticus 23 and Numbers 28 and 29. List the major feasts of the annual Hebrew calendar. In a short paragraph, describe your impression of the role that the Feast of Tabernacles played in the whole festal year.

 CREATIVE PROJECTS

1. Put the song of Moses (Psalm 90:5-12) to music by writing a tune and rewriting the lyrics as needed, keeping the meaning but creating rhyme and/or meter as desired. In a paragraph or two, reflect on the spiritual impact of the mood that your song creates.
2. With the help of a concordance, look up all the references to "the Jews" in John's Gospel. Group these usages into three categories: (a) the religious leaders, (b) Jews in general, and (c) a subgroup of Jews other than the religious leaders. Write out a short essay describing the meaning of the term "the Jews" in John's Gospel and how John's attitude ought to affect our attitude toward Jewish people today.

We will "know His voice."

Lesson 9

The Good Shepherd on Trial

Lesson Setting

Scripture: John 9:1–10:42.

John 9:1 through 10:21 continues John's description of events that took place in the context of Jesus' visit to the Feast of Tabernacles in Jerusalem. Jesus heals a blind man (one of the more amusing stories in the Bible) and then uses that experience as a living parable to illustrate His life and teachings. In John 10:22-42 Jesus returns to the temple during the Feast of Dedication (Hanukkah, about two months later) and is accused of blasphemy. This lesson will focus particularly on the theme of the Good Shepherd.

Tuffy was the life of the party. (The Greek word for *blind man* is *tuphlos*, hence "Tuffy.") Although he had been born blind, he had also been born with a keen wit and a clever tongue. He had not yet reached his teen years when his quick comebacks and acid humor kept everyone around him in stitches. It wasn't long before he was on everybody's party list. If he wasn't in the mood to go to a particular party, the host would often slip him a few shekels to come and help entertain his guests. Since Tuffy's source of income consisted mainly of begging, he was usually happy to oblige. He called it his "night job."

But deep inside there was a lot of pain mixed in with the humor. Tuffy knew that many of the same people who laughed at his jokes despised him in their hearts. You see, many Jewish people in those days had the idea that every illness or handicap was the direct result of a specific sin. So if a child was born blind, they believed that either his parents had done something terrible, or God was punishing him in advance for sins that he himself would commit later. Even if the blind person had done nothing wrong, he or she was still tainted by bad blood and, therefore, was not worthy of respect.

One day Tuffy was begging near one of the entrances to the temple. A Rabbi and His group of students approached.

"How's it going, my friend?" the Rabbi asked kindly.

"Isn't it a little obvious?" Tuffy replied, "I was born blind. Have you ever seen a blind carpenter? Have you ever seen a blind sea captain? Have you ever seen a rabbi who was born blind? So how am I supposed to get a job? Can you help me?"

The Rabbi was chuckling quietly. "I like this guy," He said to His students.

> Has there been a time in your life when you were excluded from a group because of your religious convictions? How did it feel? How did you respond? Did this exclusion eventually prove to be a blessing, or does it continue to hurt today? Why?

Then Tuffy heard those familiar but painful words from one of the men. "Rabbi, who sinned, this man or his parents, that he was born blind?"

The Rabbi responded, "Wrong question. This blindness has nothing to do with this man's behavior or that of his parents. He is blind so that the work of God can be clearly seen in his life. Remember, I am the light of the world."

I like this guy, thought Tuffy.

He was startled by what happened next. He heard the Rabbi spit on the ground. He had heard lots of people spit on the ground when they first met him. That was a way some showed their disgust for people they despised in their hearts. Did this kind teacher say nice things then act spitefully? He sensed the Rabbi bending over. Then he heard the sound of activity on the ground at his feet. He seemed to be mixing something. Then the Rabbi straightened up. Suddenly Tuffy felt a slimy mess being spread over his eyes.

"Hey, what are you doing?" yelled Tuffy. "That stuff is gross! What are you smearing on me?"

"It will be all right," said the Rabbi. His voice still sounded kind. "Just go down to the Pool of Siloam and wash it off."

"Thanks a lot! By the time I get back, I'll have lost a day's income!" Grumpily he set off toward the Pool of Siloam, some 1,200 yards away. Behind him he could hear expressions of disgust from the students, but the Rabbi was still chuckling, as if He knew something no one else knew.

Tuffy was puzzled. Smearing muddy goo on his eyes had made him angry, yet the Rabbi seemed so kind and understanding. And he remembered the part about, "He is blind so that the work of God can be clearly seen in his life." Was something special about to happen to him? And what was this about the light of the world? Things just weren't adding up. *O well,* he thought, *first things first. Got to get this slimy stuff off my face.*

Half an hour later he reached the pool. He bent and began to wash his face, vigorously scrubbing his eyelids. Suddenly he saw a flash of . . . what? He saw something clear and liquid moving, and something else seemed to be in it. What was it? Could this be a reflection of *his* face? Suddenly it hit him, "I can see," he shouted. Then he froze. *Light of the world,* he thought. *So that's what this miracle was all about!*

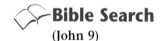 **Bible Search**

(John 9)

Read John 9 and then answer the following questions:

1. What previous theme is continued in the story of the healing of the man blind from birth?

   The healing occurred on the same day as the Abraham debate of John 8, so the background of the Feast of Tabernacles (including such themes as water and light) is still in mind.

2. Why did some Pharisees object to the healing?

3. Why did other Pharisees feel differently?

4. What did the healed man believe about Jesus?

5. What was the result of the Pharisees' investigation?
6. How does Jesus apply the living parable of the formerly blind man's experience?
7. What did Jesus mean by the reversal of verse 39?

This amusing story functions as a living parable. By healing the man, Jesus illustrated the truth of His earlier statement, "I am the light of the world." As the Light of the world, Jesus brings physical sight to a man who was born blind. But there is a deeper meaning behind this story.

The healing creates a serious dilemma for the Pharisees. On the one hand, the healing points to the work of a man approved by God. But by a nonemergency healing on the Sabbath, Jesus appears to be acting like a false prophet (Deuteronomy 13:1-5). The humor of the story lies in its biting irony. The man who was blind sees more and more clearly that Jesus represents the true God of Israel. On the other hand, the Pharisees, who see clearly in the physical sense, and who are supposed to be the guardians of the faith of Israel, become increasingly blind to the truth about Jesus (John 9:41).

Jesus' healing of the blind man, therefore, becomes symbolic of His ability to bring spiritual *in-sight*, while the Pharisees' rejection of the healing symbolizes their rejection of the truth about God, which Jesus brought into the world. The unbelief of the Pharisees is amazing to the man (John 9:30), especially since they admit that the miracle actually occurred (John 9:34). Their rejection is rooted in their willful blindness with regard to the claims of Jesus.

Even today, few people reject Jesus out of a lack of evidence. Usually they reject Him out of an unwillingness to let Him "tamper" with their lifestyle. It is easy to find excuses not to believe when we are protecting some cherished sin or attitude. The root reality of the unbeliever is unconfessed and unforsaken sin. These things "blind" one to the truths about Jesus.

 **Journaling**
(Experience)

In what areas of my spiritual life right now am I being "blinded" to God's will for me? Are there cherished sins or attitudes that I am trying to protect? What steps can I take to deal with these things?

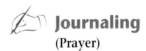 **Journaling**
(Prayer)

Give me clear spiritual vision, so I can . . .

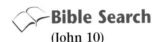 **Bible Search**
(John 10)

Verses 35-41 of chapter 9 set the stage for the Good Shepherd discourse of John 10. Jesus cares for the outcasts. When the leaders of a religious system cast people out on the basis of the leaders' enmity for Jesus, they demonstrate their own blindness (John 9:39-41) and give Jesus the opportunity to collect these outcasts for Himself (John 9:35-38).

The story about the shepherd and the sheep in John 10:1-5 is the closest thing to a parable that you can find in the Gospel of John. Actually this "figure of speech" (John 10:6) bears a lot of similarity with ancient riddles.

Read John 10:1-21 and answer the following questions:

8. What is the proper way to enter a sheep pen?

9. What kind of people climb in some other way?

10. Why do the sheep follow the shepherd?

11. How does Jesus describe Himself in John 10:7, 9?

12. Whom does Jesus describe as thieves and robbers?

13. What is the Good Shepherd willing to do?

Sheep pens in ancient Palestine were usually natural caves. The sheep would be led into the cave in the evening, and the shepherd would take his position at the entrance to the cave and sleep there. Any robber or wild animal that sought access to the sheep would have to physically get past the shepherd to do it. Where caves were not available, a fieldstone enclosure would be built with an opening at one end just big enough for the shepherd to block with his body as he slept. So when Jesus described Himself as the Good Shepherd and as the Gate for the sheep, listeners would have recognized that these concepts were two different ways of describing the same activity.

When threats to the sheep would come, therefore, the shepherd might easily feel called on to risk his life in order to protect the sheep, especially if he is the owner of the sheep. This stands in contrast to the thieves and robbers, who are only seeking a fast buck or a quick meal.

14. What kind of shepherd tends to abandon the sheep when he sees a wolf coming?

15. What other part of the Gospel is especially in view as Jesus describes Himself as the Good Shepherd?

16. How capable is the Good Shepherd of protecting His sheep?

17. What kind of life does the Good Shepherd offer?

 **Journaling**

(Insight)

How do John 9 and 10 enhance my understanding of Jesus, myself, others?

Jesus Is the Good Shepherd

When Jesus describes Himself as the Gate through which the sheep must pass in order to be saved, He is delivering the same message as Acts 4:12 ("Salvation is found in no one else") and John 14:6 ("I am the way and the truth and the life"). Now that He has come, Jesus declares that there is no other means of salvation. There is no other way into the sheepfold, except by the Gate. As the Gate of salvation, Jesus is the one who brings people to the Father. Eternal life is found in relationship with Jesus Christ (John 17:3).

As the Good Shepherd, Jesus is the One who takes care of those who have entered the sheep pen of the church. His two great qualifications for being the Good Shepherd are (1) that He is willing to lay down His life for the sheep (John 10:11-13, 17, 18) and (2) that He understands sheep (John 10:3, 14-16). Their welfare is His primary concern.

Verse 21 clearly ties this part of the Gospel back to chapter 9. In John 10:1-21 Jesus is the Good Shepherd who heals the blind man and then rescues him from the spiritual abuse of the religious leaders. The blind man of John 9, in turn, was a sheep that recognized the voice of the Good Shepherd (John 10:4).

Jesus contrasts the Good Shepherd with two other types of people who relate to sheep. One type is the thieves and robbers. These invest nothing in the sheep; they are interested only in what they can gain for themselves. Jesus probably had in mind the chief priests of the temple, who put on a show of piety in order to receive the offerings and fees that the worshipers brought to the temple with them.

The other contrasting type is the hired hand, who doesn't own the sheep, and, therefore, has no personal concern for them. He watches them only to make a living. When a wild animal comes, he protects himself rather than the sheep. Jesus probably had in mind the Pharisees of chapter 9. Although the Pharisees were much more involved in the needs and concerns of the people than the chief priests were, they did not truly care for the sheep. They did not know them intimately, nor were they willing to lay down their lives, or even their reputations, for the sheep.

As the Good Shepherd, Jesus claimed the outcasts of the religious leaders for Himself (John 9:34-38). The figure of speech in John 10, therefore, operates at two levels. In its original telling, it was a rebuke to the religious leaders of John 9:40, who, in their rough handling of the man born blind, betrayed their true character as hired hands. At the extended level of the gospel itself, the story functioned to encourage the second generation, which faced treatment similar to that experienced by the man born blind.

In Matthew 18 the parable of the lost sheep functions differently; it is concerned with church discipline. The shepherd in Matthew 18 is the elder or pastor of the church. As a true follower of Jesus, the elder will do whatever it takes to find a sheep that has drifted out of the church (Matthew 18:12, 13). But sometimes the elders of a church simply function as "authorities" who don't respond to the sheep the way God does; instead, they love to censure the "little ones" in the church who struggle with weaknesses and immaturity (Matthew 18:5-7, 10). Jesus warns those in authority that one day they will be called into a higher court.

In Luke 15:3-7 the sheep is not thrown out; it wanders out all by itself. Yet the Good Shepherd goes out to find it anyway. The message of John 10 is, "I don't let my sheep get lost" (John 10:28, 29). The message of Luke 15 is, "Even if they choose to get lost, I never give up on them. I will do whatever it takes to find them and bring them back."

Journaling
(Experience)

In what ways am I like the wandering sheep, the thieves and robbers, and/or the hired hands in this passage?

I Wanna Be a Sheep

The Good Shepherd passage offers two powerful messages that can guide our lives today. First, as the Good Shepherd, Jesus offers everything we need for an abundant life (John 10:10). He promises that we will "know his voice." Those who commit everything to Jesus receive the privilege of deep and intimate relationship that grows and grows. He is the caring friend who will never leave us or forsake us. He will guide us in our thoughts and impressions. And He will provide life to the full, an abundance of meaning, joy, and fulfillment.

Second, those who are in relationship with Jesus are called to be undershepherds. This calling is not reserved only for pastors and elders. It is the privilege of everyone who is in relationship with Jesus (Matthew 28:19, 20). He invites us to have the same kind of caring concern for others as the Good Shepherd has for His sheep. The one who truly cares about classmates and friends will never be pushy and abusive (as the Pharisees were in John 9), but will seek to act out of caring concern for the benefit of others. The world is full of sorrow, crying, pain, and dying. There is a continual need for people who, out of the strength they have received in Christ, will reach out to build up and encourage others. Such undershepherds will find that meeting the needs of others out of genuine love is what brings with it the deepest level of joy and fulfillment.

Anchor Text

"I am the good shepherd. The good shepherd lays down his life for the sheep" (John 10:11).

Reaction

Discussion Questions

1. What ideas would the second generation of Christians have received from the story about the man who was born blind?

2. In what ways do people today stigmatize others because of their ancestry or family background?

3. Why couldn't Jesus have waited until another day to heal the man born blind? What point do you think He was trying to make about Sabbath keeping?

4. How does one sense the "voice" of Jesus today? How can we follow a voice that we cannot hear audibly?

5. Why does religion provide such a fertile ground for money-making schemes? How can people protect themselves against getting bilked by religious frauds?

6. In what ways are sheep like or unlike human beings? Which aspect of sheep behavior is most likely to have caused Jesus to draw the analogy He did?

Expanded Horizons

1. Use the two-page worksheet "Healing of the Blind Man" provided by your teacher to record information about the reactions of individuals to Jesus.

2. Compare John 10:1-21 with Matthew 18:10-14 and Luke 15:3-7 on the worksheet "The Lost Sheep Motif" provided by your teacher.

God gave us faces; we create our own impressions.

Lesson 10

The Therapy of Thankfulness

Lesson Setting

Scripture: John 11:1-57.

John 11 divides naturally into two parts. First, there is the story about the death and resurrection of Lazarus (John 11:1-44). This astounding miracle proves that Jesus is truly the Resurrection and the Life (John 11:25, 26). In reaction to the same miracle, however, the religious leaders lay specific plans to kill Him in order, they feel, to save the nation from destruction (John 11:45-57).

E motions—can you trust them? Feelings—do they give a reliable picture of reality? They certainly seem to. I am what is known as a "night person." That means I'm wide awake in the evening but in another universe in the morning. If you call me at 5:30 in the morning, I'm likely to snarl, and I may even bark. But even more likely, I will put the earpiece to my mouth and the mouthpiece to my ear and wonder why we have such a lousy connection!

Along with this zombielike condition comes a feeling of depression some mornings. I feel like I'm no good to anybody, I'm a failure at all that I do, and nobody loves me. The amazing thing is that if I get out of bed and get going, these feelings will pass in a few minutes. Were those depressed feelings a picture of reality? No, they are only the product of chemicals in the brain that follow a daily cycle. Feelings can be as fickle as the weather in Seattle. They can, nevertheless, be very convincing.

A good example of a highly emotional person is Mary of Bethany. Her life, as we glimpse it in the Bible, is one of many ups and downs. Her feelings sometimes mirror reality and sometimes do not. Her relationship with Jesus has ups and downs too. Things didn't start out too well. Her first encounter with Jesus is not mentioned in Scripture, unless it is portrayed anonymously in John 8:1-11. But the Bible tells us that Mary was a "sinner" (Luke 7:37-39). In its context, the term *sinner* implies sexual sin, probably prostitution. But at some point Mary came face to face with Jesus. I picture her falling down at His feet. Her feelings? Humiliation, guilt, self-hatred. But she sensed in Jesus a man she could trust. He knew her sinfulness, yet He loved and accepted her. A healing process began.

The second encounter finds her, again, at

> Make a list of five things you are thankful for right now. List them in order of importance to you. Share the top two items on the list with a classmate.

89

the feet of Jesus, this time basking in His presence. Martha is in the kitchen, and Mary is listening to Jesus. Here the emotions are upbeat. The scene is one of joy and contentment. Why? She had that one thing that is needed, a close personal friendship with Jesus (Luke 10:42). Her feelings were under control and in tune with Jesus. Now that she had accepted Jesus—she would never be depressed again, right? Wrong!

One day her brother Lazarus got sick. . . .

 Bible Search
(John 11:1-44)

Read John 11:1-44 and then answer the following questions:

1. What message do Mary and Martha send to Jesus?
2. How does Jesus respond?
3. What is the situation when Jesus finally arrives in Bethany?
4. How do the two sisters react to the news of Jesus' arrival outside town?
5. What do the sisters know about Jesus that tried their faith?

Jesus' action in staying away from Bethany may seem cruel and unusual. But in the Gospel of John, Jesus never does anything apart from the direction of God. His whole mission in life is to bring glory to God (John 11:4).

There may have been a hidden motive in Jesus' action. In popular Jewish belief at that time, the soul of an individual hovered over the body for three days after death, hoping for resuscitation to take place. After that, there was no more hope of resurrection. Had Jesus come earlier, His raising of Lazarus from the dead might not have had the impact that it came to have. But this outcome was not discernible to Jesus' friends in advance.

Looked at from the perspective of Mary and Martha, the death of Lazarus was not the worst thing. The worst part about the situation was that Jesus delayed in coming! Suppose your brother (or sister or best friend or parent) was dying, and your doctor had the ability to save his life; but he refused to come until after the Super Bowl—causing your brother to die. How would you feel? Angry? Resentful? Depressed? All of the above and more?

Martha "went out to meet him, but Mary stayed at home" (John 11:20). Perhaps Mary didn't *feel* like seeing Jesus just then. Fragile Mary was certainly feeling hurt. The Man she had trusted seemed to have let her down. Why? Maybe He had rejected her. Maybe He was tired of her moods. Maybe their entire friendship had been a mistake!

Had Christ been in the sickroom, Lazarus would not have died; for Satan would have had no power over him. . . . Therefore Christ remained away. He suffered the enemy to exercise his power, that He might drive him back, a conquered foe. He permitted Lazarus to pass under the dominion of death; and the suffering sisters saw their brother laid in the grave. Christ knew that as they looked on the dead face of their brother their faith in their Redeemer would be severely tried. But He knew that because of the struggle through which they were now passing their faith would shine forth with far greater power (*The Desire of Ages*, 528).

6. What does Martha say that made it clear that she had not lost hope?

The expression in verse 27 matches what the writer of the Gospel sought to elicit from his readers as expressed in the Gospel's statement of purpose in John 20:31.

7. When does Mary finally go to Jesus?
8. When Mary finally meets Jesus, does she offer similar expressions of faith to those that Martha expressed?
9. How does Jesus respond to Mary's arrival statement?

Relationships are such fragile things. Jesus is in the park outside of town; Mary is in the house. Both seem to be waiting for some kind of signal. This is a picture of reality. Jesus is always there, standing in the shadows of our lives, waiting to be invited in. Sometimes, like Mary, our eyes are so blinded with tears that we can't see Him standing there with arms outstretched. Sometimes our ears are so deaf with anger, grief, or pain that we can't hear Him inviting us to come. At such times He sends a representative, someone with feelings and flesh who can press home the invitation.

Fragile Mary falls again at the feet of Jesus. She repeats Martha's complaint, but without any affirmation of continued faith. As a result, she receives no revelation from Jesus, and He draws no expression of faith from her (compare with John 11:25-27). Instead, He is deeply troubled at her apparent lack of faith and that of those with her.

Jesus has come to invite them to behold the resurrection and the life, but their minds are fixed on their loss instead.

But Jesus speaks no words of rejection. Mary is back where she belongs, accepted at the feet of Jesus. She is apparently still resentful, still insecure, still a raging sea of turbulent feelings. But Jesus doesn't walk away. He doesn't chide her for her feelings. He accepts her as she is. Her feelings do not in any way cause Him to change course. He doesn't refuse to perform the wonderful surprise that He has planned for her.

 **Journaling**
(Experience)

Recall times in your life when God delayed answering your prayer requests. How did each delay affect your faith at the time? In what way is your current faith still colored by those events?

 **Journaling**
(Insight)

In what ways are you like Mary? Martha? The disciples in this story?

Gaining Control Over Our Emotions

Why do our emotions have such a powerful effect upon us? One very important reason is that by nature human beings are absorbed in themselves. As important as it is to spend time in thoughtful reflection on our lives, there is a dark side to concentrating on one's own needs and feelings. This was brought home to me one day when I paid a visit to a mental hospital in New York City. The ward that I visited was filled with people in various stages of detachment from reality. But there was one thing that all of the patients who could communicate had in common. Every sentence was centered around the word *I.* Every conversation had one subject and only one. The common denominator of mental illness seems to be an extreme focus on self. Self-centeredness is the path to self-destruction. A self-centered person will always be a prisoner of his or her own emotions.

There is, however, a scientifically proven way to gain control of our feelings that is also compatible with the Bible. Ellen G. White describes it well in *The Ministry of Healing*, 251. "It is a law of nature that our thoughts and feelings are encouraged and strengthened as we give them utterance." Talk doubt, and you will have more doubt. Talk discouragement, and you will have more discouragement. But the reverse is also true. Talk faith, and you will have more faith. Talk thankfulness, and you will have joy. To quote Ellen G. White again from the same page: "Nothing tends to promote health of body and of soul more than does a spirit of gratitude and praise."

A spirit of gratitude and praise is the ideal antidote to self-absorption and the depression that comes with it. Words of thankfulness and praise take our minds off ourselves and direct them toward Jesus.

Gail was having major difficulties with a classroom full of young children. Her life had been an unending series of disappointments. She felt like a failure and was in a state of continual depression. A preacher named Glenn Coon suggested a remedy for both the class and her depression.

He encouraged her to each morning think of, and write down, a list of ten things that she was thankful for or should be thankful for. She was to take the list with her throughout the day and review the list as often as possible, preferably every half-hour to an hour. The objects on the list were to be practical, everyday-type realities like air, sunlight, forgiveness, the color of the carpet, the cat, etc. She was to incorporate each item into a sentence prayer, such as "Thank You, Lord, for air. Thank You, Lord, for forgiveness. Thank You, Lord, for the cat, etc." The secret to the system, Coon suggested, was to say these sentences out loud whenever possible. The next best thing would be to say them in the mind. Expression would deepen impression.

Now when Gail first heard this suggestion, she thought the idea was pretty stupid but decided to try it out on the class anyway. If it worked for them, it might work for her as well. So she offered a special prize to each child who would bring a list of ten things they were thankful for each day until school closed. With twelve weeks of school left, that meant they would have to find 600 different things to be thankful for. She did not even ask the children to repeat the lists or pray sentence prayers using them. They were just to bring a new list every day. Soon the whole atmosphere in the school changed. Problem children began working like honor students. The classroom became a pleasant place.

Something else happened. Parents began to help their children find and write up their lists day by day. The parents themselves, including a number of grumpy men and women, became happier and more cooperative. The school and church were becoming a little bit of heaven on earth.[1]

At first hearing, this "thank therapy" may sound simplistic, but it really works. Try it; you'll like it. But what if you run out of things to put on the list each morning? Open a dictionary and you will find items on every page, sometimes dozens, for which to be thankful. It is amazing how many things God has done for us, and yet we rarely take the opportunity to thank Him, to our own physical and mental loss.

I'll never forget the time I was preaching a sermon entitled "Dealing With Depression." The day before I was to preach, I experienced what in my career has been the ultimate betrayal. A leader in the church threatened my career in a way that to me seemed unjust. I was forced to call all my hopes and dreams into question. This sent me into a huge emotional tailspin that made the very act of preaching a painful physical challenge.

When I got up to speak, I was depressed. It was as if a gray Michigan cloud had settled over my head, blotting the congregation from my view. But I spoke of the power of gratitude and praise. I showed how we can thank Jesus in every circumstance, no matter how trying. As I taught the people how to praise Him for life, breath, water, and mercy, my own cloud lifted as the Son of Righteousness filled my own soul. It is impossible to estimate the power that gratitude and praise have on our emotions. Expression deepens impression. As we learn to praise and thank God for everything, our emotions become more and more harnessed in devotion to Him.

 Journaling
(Prayer)

Make a list of ten specific things that you are thankful to God for. Incorporate these into a series of sentence prayers as illustrated in the above narrative.

Bible Search
Sometimes It Takes a Miracle

While thankfulness and praise can make a huge difference in the way we feel, no amount of thankfulness and praise, in themselves, could have brought Lazarus back from the dead. The only hope for one who had been dead four days was the Godlike, life-giving power of Jesus.

Answer the following questions on the basis of the texts cited:

10. What does Jesus command as He approaches the tomb? John 11:39.

    Although Martha had expressed faith in Jesus earlier, even her faith wavers as she comes face to face once more with the finality of the tomb.

11. With what words does Jesus perform the miracle? John 11:43.

    Lazarus responds by shuffling out in his grave clothes, the only "mummy" who ever truly walked. In a scene garnished by John with a little humor, Jesus orders them to "untie the prisoner and let him go."

12. Do the religious leaders believe in the reality of what Jesus did? John 11:47.

13. How do the religious leaders respond? John 11:53; 12:9-11.

An atheist, commenting publicly on this text, noted that Jesus called Lazarus by name "in a loud voice." He suggested that Lazarus was not really dead and that he and Jesus staged the resurrection to substantiate Jesus' claims for Himself. Jesus used the loud voice and mentioned Lazarus by name as a prearranged signal that it was time for Lazarus to come out.

A little old lady in the crowd stood up and offered a different interpretation. "If Jesus hadn't called Lazarus by name," she said, "every dead person in that entire cemetery would have come forth."

The bottom line of Christian faith is that there is real power in the gospel. That power that raised Lazarus and Jesus from the dead is real, and it is still available today. Even today, there are times when only a miracle can clear away the clouds. We will all have

Reaction

Discussion Questions

1. Which of the two women in John 11 would the second generation of Christians be more likely to identify with, Mary or Martha? Why?

2. How do you think Jesus' delay in going to Bethany affected His disciples? The other Jews in the story?

3. Based on the evidence of this chapter, how would you describe the personalities of Mary and Martha respectively?

4. Since Jesus knows that He has come to raise Lazarus from the dead, why do you think He is so troubled and sorrowful in verses 33-38?

5. Would the concerns of the religious leaders in John 11:45-57 have been legitimate if Jesus had been a fraud? Explain your answer.

Expanded Horizons

1. Make a list of ten new things to be thankful for each class day during the next two weeks of this unit. At least two times during these two weeks, take time to review and pray over your lists. Write in one or two paragraphs any changes you experience as a result of this "therapy."

2. In the Bible, at least ten different individuals were raised from the dead. As a whole class (with the help of concordances and/or Bible dictionaries, as needed) find and list all these resurrec-

the John 11 experience at one time or another. Death, betrayal, loss, and destruction may leave a real sense of loss that cannot be explained away. No amount of thankfulness and praise may at times be able to undo a reality that cannot be glossed over or explained away. But at such points we can remember that the God who raised Jesus from the dead can still create something out of nothing. Even when all seems hopeless, we can still put our trust in Him.

Anchor Text

"Jesus said to her, 'I am the resurrection and the life. He who believes in me will live, even though he dies' " (John 11:25).

Endnotes

1. The story about Gail and the principles of thank therapy (tested by the author of this unit for over twenty years) can be found in Glenn and Ethel Coon's book *The Lovely Lord of the Lord's Day* (Nampa, Idaho: Pacific Press Publishing Association, 1976).

tion accounts. How many eras of biblical history experienced resurrections? Study the biblical texts gathered by the class and then write a paragraph or two describing the significance of those features of the Lazarus narrative that you consider special or unique.

CREATIVE PROJECTS

1. Start a "Good Stuff" club at your school (come up with a better name for it too), designed to celebrate all the "good stuff" that God does for us day by day. Challenge your friends and teachers to practice listing ten things they are thankful for every day. Have club members identify themselves by a signal and/or a logo. Whenever club members meet, they can snap, "What are you thankful for right now?" or "Gimme the Good Stuff" and expect an immediate answer. Rewards (for having thankfulness on the mind) and "punishments" (for forgetting to) can be part of the fun. At the end of the unit, write a two- to three-page essay on the benefits of being part of a group of thankful people.
2. Briefly describe a strategy for elevating feelings of depression.

Kindness permeates a life like expensive perfume.

Lesson 11

Devoted Soul

Lesson Setting

Scripture: John 12:1-50.

John 12 contains two main parts. The first (verses 1-36) involves a series of events that set the Gospel stage for the crucifixion of Jesus. The rest of John 12 (verses 37-50) marks the end of Jesus' public ministry and, therefore, functions as a summary epilogue of some of the key themes developed in the first 12 chapters of the Gospel. The focus of this lesson is on the change that came over Mary of Bethany after Jesus raised her brother from the dead.

Mary stood in the shadows at the edge of the room, her heart once more filled with emotion as she contemplated this gathering of the most important people in her life. The others in the room were too busy enjoying the party to take notice of her quiet reverie.

There was Martha, bustling in and out of the room, preparing food, serving, and directing helpers with her usual efficiency. Good old Martha, a little uptight maybe, but you could always count on her to be there when you needed somebody. And how she could cook! She had been really pleasant since their brother Lazarus had been raised from the dead.

O yes, Lazarus. Mary's eyes moved to the center of the room where Lazarus was reclining, the guest of honor along with Jesus.

Mary never tired of gazing at his wonderful face, the dear brother she had given up for lost. Her eyes followed every movement of his mouth as he explained over and over what it felt like to be wrapped like a mummy. Life was good!

Her eyes moved from Lazarus to Jesus. Wonderful, wonderful Jesus! Her face beamed with joy as she gazed on His animated face, telling stories while projecting kindness with His eyes. Was it possible to love anyone more than she loved Jesus? Her heart began to pound with excitement as she reached under her outer garment and felt the flask of expensive perfume, worth a whole year's wages. Jesus was worth any gift, any sacrifice. How could she ever have doubted Him? She remembered the look on His face when she had chided Him for not coming to Bethany sooner when Lazarus had died. It wasn't so much hurt as . . . disappointment. Well,

Have you ever cared deeply about someone, but you were afraid to let him or her know? Why did you find it so difficult to share your feelings?

she would never disappoint Him again!

She had heard disturbing rumors about plots to kill Jesus. Lazarus had even told her that Jesus believed that He would be killed on his next trip to Jerusalem. Mary wasn't much for flowers at funerals; she liked to do her giving while people were still alive to appreciate it. She felt convinced that this was the time and place to demonstrate her devotion to Jesus. It might be her last chance. But in front of all these people?

Her gaze fell upon Simon, the host, and she wavered. Simon was the head elder at the synagogue. He, more than anyone else except Jesus, knew all about her sinful past. He knew about the prostitution that had provided the money for the very perfume she now clutched beneath her robe. She and Simon also knew something no one else knew. He had been the first. He was the one who had cast a long glance at her over the potluck table years before. He was the one who used his spiritual stature to charm and overwhelm a vulnerable young woman. He was the one who started her down the road to destruction from which Jesus eventually saved her.

For some reason, though, Mary never felt angry at Simon. As she gazed into his face just then, she felt no anger, only shame. He was a good man, the leader of the synagogue. Surely it was her fault somehow that he had transgressed with her. That's why she had never exposed him—she blamed herself. Her heart filled with shame as she realized how unworthy she was to honor Jesus. What if everybody laughed when she anointed Jesus? What if Simon called the

police like the time . . . Mary shuddered and moved deeper into the shadows, seeking a way to sneak from the room and head home for a good cry.

But wait. . . . Hadn't she confessed her sins to Jesus (being careful not to name Simon)? Hadn't He accepted her? If Jesus accepted her, did it really matter what anyone else thought? Hadn't He told her how valuable she was to God? Her courage began to rise as she remembered all the affirmation she had received from Jesus, as she recalled the amazing changes Jesus had brought into her life. She loved Him with every fiber of her being. She would do anything, go anywhere for Jesus. She would die for Him if need be. Why should she hesitate now just because Simon was there?

Her thoughts evoked once more the rumors about Jesus' impending death. Her jaw set with determination. Holding the precious flask of perfume, she began to move decisively toward the center of the room. . . .

Bible Search
(John 12:1-12)

Read John 12:1-12 and then answer the following questions:

1. When and where did the event of 12:1-12 take place?

    This dinner probably took place Saturday night, the week before the crucifixion. The town is located about two miles east of Jerusalem, on the other side of the Mount of Olives.

2. How much perfume did Mary pour on Jesus' feet?

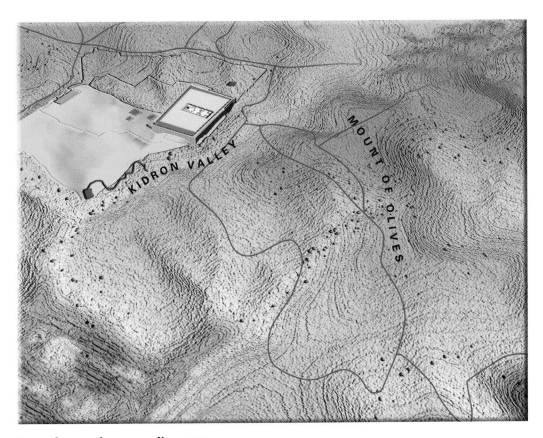

Jerusalem and surrounding area

3. Was Mary able to do this act without drawing attention to what she had done?

4. How did Judas react to Mary's act of devotion?

5. What did Jesus say in response to Judas?

One of the striking characteristics of John's Gospel is the author's subtle use of irony. This ironic humor reaches a high point in John 11 and 12. For example, the religious leaders lament in 11:48 that if they don't put an end to Jesus' work, "everyone will believe in him, and then the Romans will come and take away both our place and our nation." Caiaphas, a blustering braggart ("You know nothing at all!"—11:49), comes on the scene to argue that the council has to do away with Jesus if the nation is to survive.

John acknowledges that Caiaphas accurately prophesied (in hostility to Jesus, of course) that Jesus' death would save the nation (11:51). But what does the reader at the end of the century already know? That in crucifying Jesus, the ruling council brought upon themselves the very consequences they feared. Because they crucified

Jesus, the whole world became aware of the salvation Jesus brought, and the Romans destroyed the city and temple anyway.

The heart of the narrative at the beginning of John 12 lies in the deliberate contrast between Mary's wholehearted faith in and love for Jesus and the coldhearted calculations of Caiaphas (at the end of chapter 11) and Judas (in the context of the story). Judas becomes the object of a subtle yet penetrating irony. He claims that the expenditure of perfume as an anointing for burial is a wasteful act (12:5), yet by betraying Jesus, he is the one largely responsible for its necessity. Judas expresses concerns for the poor, yet in stealing from the purse, he makes it clear that the only poor person he cares about is himself (verses 5, 6). Later on in the Gospel, the disciples think that Judas is leaving the upper room to give something to the poor (13:29) when, in fact, he is going out to betray Jesus for a price (13:21, 26, 27, 30).

Judas becomes the foil to Mary's soul devotion in the narrative. Mary's anointing of Jesus' feet is motivated by unselfish love and sacrifice. Judas's criticism of Mary, on the other hand, is motivated by greed and deceit. Once again, Jesus demonstrates that He knows what is in the heart of another person, but He does not expose Judas's motivations to public view. Instead, He defends Mary by pointing out that social action (helping the poor), as important as that may be, is ultimately meaningless apart from the Cross (12:7, 8). However, instead of learning that honoring Jesus is far more valuable than money, Judas is soon to exchange

Jesus' life for thirty pieces of silver.

Mary Devoted Her Soul

In this scene we see Mary's total devotion of soul. Every emotion trembles with gratitude to the One who is about to die for her. The perfume she pours on Jesus had cost her a year of work (albeit humiliating and shameful work), but it represents her whole life, gratefully offered to Jesus. Such total devotion is rarely popular, as Judas's reaction makes clear. "What a waste," people say. "You could have done great things with your money, but you chose to waste it on Jesus!"

To human reasoning, Mary seems emotionally disturbed. A devoted soul makes us uncomfortable.

Judas's reaction is a human response. Mary's action **does** seem a waste. What church board would approve such an expenditure? To human reasoning, Mary seems emotionally disturbed. A devoted soul makes us uncomfortable. But notice again how Jesus felt about it, this time as recorded in Mark 14:6-9: "She has done a beautiful thing to me. . . . She did what she could. . . . I tell you the truth, wherever the gospel is preached throughout the world, what she has done will also be told, in memory of her." Mary was one of just a few who comforted Jesus on the cross. In this verse we see how Jesus treasures the devoted soul. How many times I wish I could have comforted Him on the cross. How gladly I would wipe His brow, carry His cross, speak an encouraging word. If only I . . . well, she did! Can we comfort Jesus today? Hebrews tells us that it is possible for human beings to crucify the Son of God afresh (Hebrews 6:4-6). If that is true, then we can also comfort Him afresh! We can comfort Him in the wholehearted devotion of all our feelings to Him. When we love Him, praise Him, cherish Him, it makes a difference to Him!

How can you and I develop a devotion like Mary's? First, a devoted soul comes only in response to another devoted soul. We love Him because He first loved us. We forgive others because we have been forgiven. It was the Cross of Jesus that became the focus of Mary's emotions. As she came to understand what Jesus had done for her and the value that she had in His eyes, she responded.

Second, as we learn that expression deepens impression (as outlined in the previous lesson), we will spend more time expressing faith and less time expressing doubt, more time expressing thankfulness and less time expressing disappointment, more time expressing encouragement and less time expressing condemnation. As we train ourselves to obey Him in our conscious expressions, our emotions and our reactions will more and more reflect devotion to Him.

Finally, pray for total devotion to Jesus. Even the best of us find ourselves divided in our affections at times. Take hold of that small part of you that desires to be fully devoted to the Lord. Encourage it, pray about it, offer it to God (see Romans 6:11-14 for a clear and practical expression of this principle), and that part of you will grow stronger and stronger until it becomes the dominating attitude of your life. Let me illustrate this from my own experience.

I was a single pastor in New York City. One day a beautiful girl entered my congregation. She had come from North Dakota to get away from her problems. It wasn't long before New York City began to look like one *big* problem to her. After a while she decided to see if religion could help. As a conscientious pastor, of course, I arranged to study the Bible with her, three or four times a week! It was not long before my plans for her went far beyond her baptism. As our relationship grew, however, it was clear that there was a problem. She could not stand the city that I loved. Her heart longed for the flat, treeless plains of her home state.

Within a short time, word came that her great-grandfather had died. She and her mother borrowed money to purchase one-way tickets to the funeral. At the airport I had the distinct impression that she didn't plan to return. I feebly offered to pay their trip back if they wanted. When the plane was gone, I went out into the darkness of soul. For days I was angry with God. "Why did you tease me like this and then take her away?" On my knees I begged God to bring her back to me even if it wasn't His will. "Not your will but mine be done, O Lord," I prayed in essence. I was a turbulent sea of seething emotions.

In the midst of my darkness a still, small voice said, "If it's not God's will, such a marriage will never work."

"I don't care. I want her," I replied. Gradually 20 percent of me learned to pray that God's will be done, while 80 percent wanted her at any cost. Amazingly, as I continued to pray, God's will increased in importance for me. A few days later it seemed that 40 percent of me wanted God's will, and 60 percent wanted mine.

Soon after, I was on my knees at 11:00 P.M., pleading with God for a new heart. Suddenly it happened. I knew I wanted God's will more than anything. I prayed, "Thank You, Lord, for changing me. Do Your will, whatever it is. If she never comes back, I will praise Your name anyway. No matter what, Lord, do Your will with me." A tremendous sense of peace and assurance came over me. My whole soul was dedicated to Him. At the very instant I said Amen in my mind, the phone rang. It was a collect call from Pam. She wanted to know if I was still interested in sending plane tickets to her! That was more than twenty-five years ago. She has been my treasure and my joy ever since.

God is often willing to give us the desires of our hearts if we will only devote ourselves fully to Him, as Mary did. Although our feelings are naturally up and down, by His grace they can be more and more devoted to Him. The God who transformed Mary still lives today and longs for our devotion. There is no greater joy than to respond to such a love!

 **Journaling**
(Experience)

What percentage of your current budget reflects a commitment to honoring Jesus? Would the percentage be different if you were a millionaire?

 **Journaling**
(Insight)

Consider Mary's depth of devotion and possible parallel actions in today's world.

 **Journaling**
(Prayer)

Pray for the total devotion Mary had.

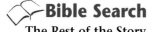 **Bible Search**
The Rest of the Story

Read John 12:12-50 and then answer the following questions:

6. What incident provided the context for the triumphal entry of Jesus into Jerusalem in John 12:10-17?

7. When the people acclaimed Jesus as He rode to Jerusalem on the donkey, what did they say about Him?

With the triumphal entry, we see the third of three reactions to the miracle of raising Lazarus from the dead. The miracle makes the religious leaders want to kill Jesus for fear of what will happen to them if they don't. The miracle fills Mary with gratitude and devoted, self-sacrificing love. At the same time, the miracle inspires the crowd to try to use Jesus to achieve their own nationalistic expectations. Of the three reactions,

Mary's is clearly the one the author of the Gospel wishes the reader to see as the great model of response to Jesus and His miraculous signs.

8. What happens next?

9. What does Jesus say in response?

This expression in John's Gospel always refers to the crucifixion of Jesus.

10. What is Jesus' strange reaction to the request of the Greeks?

11. Why is the Cross so important?

12. What is the ideal response to the Cross?

The agony of Jesus in the Garden of Gethsemane is not mentioned in the Gospel of John. But the flavor of it does occur. For some reason, the arrival of the Greeks triggers in Jesus thoughts of His death, reminiscent of the Gethsemane experience in the other Gospels.

One possible explanation of this sequence of events is that the arrival of the Greeks provided the context for a Satanic temptation. "Don't go to the Cross just yet; think of all the Greeks who need to hear the gospel first." Satan knew that the Cross was Jesus' most important act, and in many ways, he sought to deflect Jesus from it.

Following Jesus

To follow Jesus is to disown self-centeredness. When our lives are filled with striving for advantage, security, and pleasure, we do not experience the fullness of life that Jesus offers. Transferring control of our lives to Christ is the way to genuine fulfillment. Those who disown self-centeredness and submit their lives to Jesus will seek to be wherever Jesus is (John 12:26).

Where is Jesus, that we might follow Him and be where He is? The context of the passage makes it clear that Jesus is to be found in the "way of the cross" (12:23, 24, 27-33). He is found where His people are, particularly the suffering, the downtrodden, the weak, the sinner, and the outcasts. We are where He is when we follow Him and give ourselves in self-sacrificing service to those in some very down-to-earth places. The Gospel of John illustrates the believer's way of the Cross in chapter 13:1-17. As we serve others by "washing their feet," we follow Jesus in the way of the Cross. We find Him in the person of others.

Anchor Text

"You will always have the poor among you, but you will not always have me" (John 12:8).

Reaction

Discussion Questions

1. The actions of both Mary and Judas in 12:1-9 could be evil or commendable, depending on the context in which they occurred. Why do you suppose Jesus commended Mary and condemned Judas on this occasion?

2. If you had a year's worth of salary or a year of time to use to honor Jesus, how would you use it? How would your friends be likely to react?

3. In your use of time and money, how do you balance the needs of others with your own needs?

4. What does the word *sacrifice* mean in a relatively wealthy society? How can one honor Jesus today in a way similar to Mary's act?

5. How does your church relate to people like Mary, who have slipped badly but want to make a fresh start? Does it make a difference if the offense is the first?

6. What is the difference between praise and flattery? Can the praise of others be positive at times in Christian experience? Under what circumstances?

7. In practical terms, how can we find Jesus in our relationships with other people? Is Jesus found only among other Christians, or can He also be found in those who reject Him? Why?

8. How can the Cross be so glorious and yet so troubling at the same time?

9. Does devotion and surrender always bring you what you desire, as it did in this lesson?

10. Does surrender always lead to success? Socially? Financially?

1. Compare John 12:12-16 with Zechariah 9, the context from which the quotation in verse 15 is drawn. Does the arrival of the Greeks in John 12:20 parallel anything in the context of Zechariah 9:9, 10? How does the Old Testament background affect your understanding of John 12:20?

2. How does the attitude of the "crowd" in John 12 compare with the attitude recorded in John 7:40-43 and 10:19-21? In what way is our relationship with Jesus a lot like the crowd's relationship in John?

Greatness is often disguised as service.

Lesson 12

Real Greatness

Lesson Setting

Scripture: John 13:1-30.

With chapter 13, the entire tone of the Gospel of John is transformed. Instead of teaching, healing, and debating in public, Jesus retires to an unspecified place (13:1, 2)—presumably the upper room mentioned in other Gospels (Matthew 26:17-19; Mark 14:12-15; Luke 22:7-12) to quietly instruct His disciples at great length.

This portion of the Gospel begins with the account of the foot washing and the identification of the one who was to betray Jesus (John 13:1-30). Jesus and Judas take opposite paths toward greatness.

Harold is a good friend of mine who happens to be an Adventist member of a private golf club in California. His gentle and winsome character has brought him into such high regard that he recently was elected president of the club. It has become a major outreach project in his life.

One day on the golf course, I learned quite a bit about his Christian character and also about the kind of people he had contact with on a day-to-day basis. A gentleman in our foursome was stuck in a sand bunker halfway between the tee and the green. He let loose with a mighty swing that resulted in a low line-drive shot. It just so happened that a rake was lying on the ground about ten feet ahead. His ball struck the rake full-force and died right on that spot. The man let out a long string of unsavory epithets.

There was a moment of profound silence. Then Harold called out from about fifty yards away, "What kind of rake did you say that was?" All four of us cracked up laughing, and the aforementioned gentleman called out sheepishly, "Sorry, Doc [Harold is a retired medical doctor]. I forgot." I thought to myself, "What a beautiful way to maintain a high standard without belittling others or acting superior!"

One golfer in particular seemed incorrigible. He had an adjective for every club, every shot, and every other golfer, none of them repeatable here. But after several years of Harold's influence, even he struggled occasionally to exercise self-control. One morning he faced a 214-yard par-three hole. He whacked a titanic hook that landed so far into the trees on the left that he was probably further from the hole than when he started. We all braced ourselves for the worst. Then he spat out in the direction of

What does the foot-washing service in your church mean to you? Do you get a spiritual boost, or do you dread its coming? Why?

the ball, "Bless you, my brother!" We almost fell over laughing.

Later that same day, the man who was then president of the club faced a crucial shot on the seventeenth hole. The game was close, and every shot counted. He studied the layout ahead, took a couple of practice swings, and carefully prepared to hit the ball. He swung a little high, and instead of moving the ball ahead, drove it into the ground. We waited in silence for the inevitable. He said nothing and prepared to swing again. This time he drove the ball even deeper into the ground! Once again he said absolutely nothing. I was amazed. It was like stubbing your toe twice on one trip across the room. Yet he said nothing (you could see on his face that it wasn't easy).

As Harold and I were leaving the clubhouse a little later, I stepped back in and went up to the man, put a hand on his shoulder, and said, "It took a really big man to do what you did on number seventeen without swearing."

I learned something interesting that day. The media makes it seem that to be a big, tough guy these days, you have to swear vigorously, recklessly showing off your anger. I saw that day that anybody can swear; the man of really strong character is the one who can face frustrating circumstances without letting loose. It is easy to swear when you stub your toe, but it takes character to smile and say something like, "Well, I'm glad that's over" or "What kind of rake did you say that was?" It takes a strong person to exercise self-control. Letting loose is the easy way, the low-class way.

Jesus made a similar point when He washed the disciples' feet.

Bible Search
The Foot Washing

It was the custom in New Testament times for people to bathe themselves before attending a feast. Upon arrival, they would not need to bathe again; they needed to have only their feet washed. The washing of the feet, then, was like a ceremony that preceded entry into the house where they were to be guests.

Read John 13:1-17 and Philippians 2:1-8; then answer the following questions:

1. As the disciples and Jesus approached the time of the Passover Feast, what did Jesus know that the disciples did not know?
2. What was on Jesus' mind as the time of His crucifixion approached?
3. What did Jesus know about Himself at this time?
4. With that thought in mind, what does Jesus do next?
5. Why does Peter protest against Jesus' washing his feet?
6. What does Jesus know about the character of those He is serving?
7. What role does the foot washing play in cleaning the whole body?
8. What is Jesus' purpose in washing the feet of the disciples?
9. How does Philippians 2:6-8 summarize the example of Jesus?
10. According to Philippians 2:5, in what aspect of our being should we follow

this example of Jesus?

11. How is humility exhibited in practice?

The distinction Jesus makes between the foot washing and the full-body bath (13:10) is instructive. The full-body bath represents the complete cleansing that a person receives at the beginning of the Christian life. Among Adventists and many other Christians, this full cleansing is represented by a full immersion into the water of baptism.

Foot washing, on the other hand, represents the Christian's ongoing need to deal with the soiling that comes from daily contact with the sinful world and its contamination. The foot is the part of the body that in ancient times came in regular contact with the earth and therefore needed continual cleansing.

The beautiful lesson that comes through in Jesus' action is that the soiling from daily living does not call our original cleansing into question. It is not necessary to be rebaptized or to start all over every time you make a mistake. One who has bathed needs only to wash the feet again! We are not in and out of God's grace several times a day. We are secure as long as we do not choose to turn away (John 10:27-29).

The image of Jesus washing the feet of His disciples represents His forgiveness of sins committed after baptism. The image of the disciples washing each others' feet signifies our willingness to forgive those daily irritations and transgressions that threaten the unity in love that Jesus purposed for His disciples (13:34, 35).

Real Greatness

It was an upstairs room. In the corner of the room there was a small table. On the table was a large pitcher full of water, a basin, and a towel. One thing was missing. There was no servant to do the foot washing. The disciples all hung around, acting as if there was nothing for them to do.

"Nice weather we've been having lately."

"Did you notice that the Tiberias Stock Exchange went down yesterday?"

"Yeah, that's the way things go sometimes."

Moments pass and nobody moved toward the table in the corner. The problem was not

so much the touching of dirty feet. The problem was that washing feet was a slave's task. Washing feet was for nobodies, for people who would never achieve greatness. The disciples all planned to be great. After all, wasn't that why they were with Jesus? Soon He would proclaim Himself king, drive out the Romans, and one of them would be right next to Jesus. Whoever took up the towel and the basin would take themselves right out of the running for that position. Better to sit around with dirty feet than admit that you were a nobody.

"Each of the disciples, yielding to wounded pride, determined not to act the part of the servant. . . . How could [Jesus] show that it is loving service, true humility, which constitutes real greatness? . . . He had a full consciousness of His divinity, but He had laid aside His royal crown and kingly robes, and had taken the form of a servant" (*The Desire of Ages*, 644, 645).

What is real greatness? Real greatness is the King of the universe walking over to the corner of a room, picking up a towel and a basin of water, and stooping down to wash the feet of an unstable disciple like Peter and a traitor like Judas. Real greatness doesn't need to brag or assert itself. It takes real greatness to exercise self-control or to take the role of a servant. It takes real greatness to do what needs to be done even if everyone

It takes real greatness to do what needs to be done even if everyone laughs at you or despises you in their hearts.

laughs at you or despises you in their hearts.

Real greatness is to have the same attitude as Jesus (Philippians 2:5), who was "in very nature God" (Philippians 2:6) yet took "the very nature of a servant" (Philippians 2:7) and "humbled himself" (Philippians 2:8). Real greatness is to "consider others better than yourselves" (Philippians 2:3). Real greatness is to follow Jesus in the path of service and humility. Real greatness is putting yourself at the "third level down"—Jesus first, others second, ourselves third.

If you and I had been in the upper room that night, would we have acted differently? If our first thought in any situation is of our own advantage and self-interest, we are pursuing a false greatness. If our first reaction to any situation is to nag, belittle, criticize, and complain, we are exhibiting the opposite of humility and real greatness. Putting other people down says, "I am better than you." Considering others better than ourselves is to uplift, encourage, and praise. In sports the most valuable player may not be the one who scores the most points but the one who encourages his or her teammates to perform at their best.

How can we develop real greatness? How can we learn to love a life of service? Certainly, not by **trying** to be humble. That usually only makes it worse. The key to developing an attitude like Christ is to focus on **Him** (Philippians 2:5). When we focus on Christ's words (John 6:63) and His life example (John 13:12-17), we become molded more and more into His image (2 Corinthians 3:18). By beholding, we become changed.

Journaling
(Insight)

Can you think of an individual in your life who illustrates in practical terms what it means to wash feet in relationships? What aspects of that person's life might serve as a model for yours?

Journaling
(Experience)

How can you put Jesus' teaching on foot washing and servanthood to practical use in at least one relationship this week?

Journaling
(Prayer)

Tell God that you are willing to become more of a servant to others; invite Him to provide the desire, the motivation, and/or the opportunities.

Bible Search
Judas: The Other Path to Greatness

Read John 13:18-30 and answer the following questions:

12. What purpose did Jesus have in predicting His betrayal?
13. How did the knowledge of His coming betrayal affect Jesus?
14. How did Jesus choose to identify the one who would betray Him?

15. What did the disciples understand Jesus to mean by His statement to Judas?

The prospect of having a high place in the new kingdom had led Judas to espouse the cause of Christ. . . . He was continually advancing the idea that Christ would reign as king in Jerusalem. . . . It was he who set on foot the project to take Christ by force and make Him king. . . . [He hoped to secure] the first position, next to Christ, in the new kingdom (*The Desire of Ages*, 718-721).

Judas chose to follow a different path to greatness than that exhibited by Christ in the foot-washing service. On this particular point, he considered himself wiser than Christ. Surely it was obvious to anyone that greatness came from power, wealth, and the esteem of others! But his logical course of action led only to personal destruction.

Judas failed to realize that anybody can be arrogant or demand to be treated as superior. Given the opportunity, anybody can spend money or command others. It takes ***real*** greatness to act the part of a servant and do tasks that others should have done. It takes real greatness to put others first, to treat others as better than yourself.

Anchor Text

"Now that I, your Lord and Teacher, have washed your feet, you also should wash one another's feet. I have set you an example that you should do as I have done for you" (John 13:14, 15).

Reaction

1. What does it mean to "wash feet" in the context of everyday life?

2. On a scale of one to ten, how does your local church's practice of the Communion service effectively carry out Jesus' command to wash each other's feet? How successfully does it carry out the example of Jesus in its relationships with people inside and outside of the church body?

3. What do you think Jesus meant when He said to Peter, "Unless I wash you, you have no part with me"?

4. What is it about Judas's taking the bread that Jesus offers that results in Satan entering into him? (John 13:27).

5. Why do you think Peter is so firmly against Jesus' washing his feet?

6. What do you think it means when it says in Philippians 2:7 that Jesus "made himself nothing"?

7. Is the typical view of greatness in today's world more like that of Jesus or Judas? How can one best present the message of Jesus to people who are accustomed to a different kind of greatness?

8. Instead of foot washing, what symbolic action can you think of that would symbolize service and humility?

Expanded Horizons

1. A. On a sheet of paper, list all the things in John 13:1-30 that Jesus knows but the disciples do not.

   B. What do you learn about Jesus from this list?

   C. Prepare a script that illustrates what Jesus knew and the significance you attach to what He knew.

2. Create a logo or a drawing that illustrates the kind of greatness Jesus taught in the foot-washing service.

113

"Peace I leave with you; my peace I give you."

Lesson 13

Sweet Sorrow

Lesson Setting

Scripture: John 13:31–16:33.

After the foot washing is finished, the shadow of the Cross looms over the room where Jesus and His disciples are reclining. The disciples begin to realize that Jesus is truly about to leave them. In John 13 through 16, Jesus delivers to His disciples a farewell discourse in which He teaches them how to live without His physical presence, just as the second generation of Christians would have to live without the physical presence of the disciples.

Since John 13:31–16:33 is a single event, primarily involving teaching on the part of Jesus, it will be treated as a whole in this unit, but in two separate ways. In this lesson, we will examine what this passage has to say about the role and fate of the disciples, who will have to carry on the work of Jesus after He leaves. In the next lesson, we will focus particularly on the five texts in this passage that relate to the work of the Holy Spirit, whom Jesus sends to be with the disciples in His place.

I t'll be better for you if I go away." Can you imagine anyone who really loves you saying such a thing? How can it be for your good when a vital piece of you has been torn away and removed from reach? "Parting is such sweet sorrow," said Shakespeare. I know about the sorrow. I'm not so sure about the sweet.

We had had a bittersweet relationship. At its best it had been very good. We had a lot of things in common. Our differences often balanced each other out. We talked easily and at great length. Our standards and tastes were similar. But there had been many hard times as well. She was easygoing, but I was not mature enough to let her be herself. I tried hard to make her into my image of the ideal woman. She tried hard to comply. But the more I succeeded in changing her, the less I liked what she had become!

That summer we decided to break up but remain friends. It didn't work well.

We couldn't stand being together, and we couldn't stand being apart. So one day she came to me with a solution to the difficulties in our relationship.

"I've decided to go back home [a country 3,000 miles away]," she said. "That way we can each start all over again."

"No way," I responded. "I'll miss you too much. I'll go crazy without you. Let's keep trying. I'm sure we can work it out."

"I don't think so," she said. "We've been trying for two years. It's just not working out."

"Aw, come on," I asserted. "Just one more chance. If you go away, my life will be ruined."

"No, it won't," she replied. "It'll be better for you if I go away. . . ."

She had a hard time convincing me.

A week later we stood in silence at the airport terminal gate. There was nothing to say. All the talking, all the crying, had left us exhausted and empty. She handed the flight attendant her boarding pass and entered the

Recall a time when someone you were very close to moved away. How did you feel when you first found out? What kinds of things did you do to cope with the absence of that friendship?

jetway. As I watched her disappear, her words kept ringing in my ears, "It'll be better for you if I go away."

I never saw her again.

 Bible Search

(John 13:12–14:31)

Jesus waited until the departure of Judas before beginning his farewell speech to the disciples (in the Greek, 13:31 begins with *therefore*). The content of the speech, all the way through chapter 16, is intended to encourage the disciples as they enter into a life without the physical presence of Jesus.

Read John 13:21–14:31 and then answer the following questions:

1. What problem are Jesus and His disciples facing?
2. How did the disciples feel about this?
3. What were the followers of Jesus to demonstrate to the whole human race by their love for one another?

To love each other as Jesus has loved us transcends secular love. People don't normally help when it isn't convenient, give when it hurts, or face ridicule and accusations without fighting back. To love as Jesus loved is so radically different that everyone will know that something special has taken place.

The ways we use to express love to other people are the ways we ourselves have experienced love. When the "love" we have received is abusive and controlling, we seek to "love" others in abusive and controlling ways. We love others as we have been loved. On the other hand, we can learn to truly love others to the extent that we have allowed ourselves to experience Jesus' love. Those who are much loved can love much.

4. What does Jesus plan to do when He goes away?
5. What is one way the disciples will be better off if Jesus goes to the Father?
6. How will they achieve the actions that Jesus promises in verse 12?
7. What else will characterize the behavior of Jesus' disciples?

Jesus is going away, and the disciples are feeling abandoned. How can they possibly continue without Him? But Jesus makes it clear that His going away to the Father will benefit them. His presence with the Father will empower their love (13:34, 35), their prayers (14:13, 14), and their obedience (14:15, 21) through the Holy Spirit, whom He will send (14:16, 17).

A key to understanding the benefit to the disciples in Jesus' departure is found in the statement that the disciples would do greater works than Jesus (14:12). How could anyone do greater works than Jesus did? The earthly Jesus was subject to human limitations. He could be in only one place at a time. When He was with the disciples, the Father could be seen only in His person (14:9). But when He went to the Father, earthly limitations were left behind. When He sent His Spirit (14:16, 17), His disciples became the agents to manifest the character of God throughout the world.

Because Jesus went to the Father and sent the Spirit, millions of disciples have extended Jesus' work throughout the world. And a central part of that greater work was the raising up of the second generation of Christians, the audience of John's Gospel.

Journaling
(Insight)

How does Jesus' concept of love compare and contrast with the concept of love portrayed on TV and movies? In my local church? Among my schoolmates? In my home and family?

Journaling
(Prayer)

Help me to truly grasp and appreciate the love that Jesus has for me. As I appreciate His love more and more, enable me to share it with those around me.

Bible Search
(John 15:1–16:33)

In chapters 15 and 16, Jesus continues the themes of the earlier discussion, but now virtually without interruption from the disciples. It is as if the disciples are so confused that the profoundly simple teachings need to be repeated over and over.

Read John 15:1–16:33 and then answer the following questions:

8. What is the purpose of the vine-and-branches analogy?
9. How does one "remain in the vine"?
10. What is the result of an obedient relationship with Jesus?
11. What term does Jesus use to describe His relationship with His followers?
12. What are the disciples likely to experience when Jesus is gone?
13. How are the disciples to cope with both the loss of Jesus' personal presence and the hatred of the world?
14. What were the disciples experiencing in the upper room with Jesus?
15. What would be the end result of Jesus' going away?

The relationship of Jesus with the Father is the model for the disciples' relationship with Jesus. Jesus loves the disciples the way the Father loves Him (John 15:9). The disciples are to obey His commands just as He obeys the commands of His Father (15:10). At the same time, the relationship of Jesus with the world is paralleled by the relationship of the disciples with unbelievers (15:18). The world's hatred of the disciples is rooted in its hatred of Jesus (15:22-25). The values of the world are often the opposite of God's values. Therefore, in a world that does not lightly tolerate threats to its control, the disciple of Jesus will often feel out of place.

For the disciples the negative experience of hatred and persecution (15:18-25; 16:1-4) is counterbalanced by the benefits that will come to them because Jesus has gone to the Father and has sent His Spirit into the world (15:26, 27; 16:7-15). The role of the Holy Spirit in the lives of both the disciples and the second generation of Christians will be dealt with in some detail in the following lesson.

Journaling
(Experience)

How is my "remaining in the Vine" affected by the choices I made in my use of time last week? In what ways did Jesus seem especially close? Distant?

Jesus Says Goodbye

In His farewell discourse, Jesus encourages His disciples by telling them that His going away will not be the end of His ministry. There will be two substitutes for the personal, physical presence of Jesus. Through the Holy Spirit, Jesus will continue to manifest Himself and His Father to them. But that is not all. As branches connected to the Vine by the Spirit, the disciples themselves will replace Jesus in the world. Through their words and their writings, they will make Jesus real to a new generation. What is particularly exciting about this concept is that in today's world, the words and actions of believers can be the clearest and often the only picture of Jesus that many people will ever see.

Why was it for the disciples' good that Jesus was going away? John 14, 15, and 16 suggest a number of reasons:

1. Jesus will send the Holy Spirit, who will not be subject to the human limitations that Jesus was. Through the Spirit, all the benefits of Jesus' ministry will continue to be theirs (see Lesson 14).

2. Through the efforts of the disciples under the influence of the Spirit, the work of Jesus would be spread throughout the world and would have an impact on every people and place (14:12).

3. Jesus' intercessory presence with the Father would empower their prayers to heights unknown to human beings before (14:13, 14).

4. The internal work of the Holy Spirit would make Jesus' kind of love real in their lives (15:12-15). This would have convincing power in the world (13:34, 35).

5. Their deeper love for Jesus and each other would empower their obedience to Jesus' commands (14:15, 21).

6. This heightened level of obedience would bring great joy even in the midst of their sorrow over Jesus' departure (15:10, 11; 16:20-22).

7. Their experience in coping with the absence of Jesus would enable them to provide a solid foundation for the second generation. Like branches on a vine, they would bring forth much fruit (15:1-8).

Although Jesus' statement "It's for your good that I am going away" was hard to accept at the time Jesus made it, time and experience have proven it to be true. So it was for me and the young woman who went home to make our lives better. I have learned that she is happily married and has been very successful in her career as well. I, too, have been richly blessed since the time she left. She was not to blame for the difficulties in our relationship, yet her selfless act resulted in benefit for both of us. Perhaps Shakespeare had it right after all, "Parting is such sweet sorrow."

 **Journaling**
(Prayer)

Lord, do whatever it takes to make Jesus more real to me.

**Anchor Text**

"It is for your good that I am going away. Unless I go away, the Counselor will not come to you; but if I go, I will send him to you" (John 16:7).

118

Reaction

Discussion Questions

1. In what ways do you think that the kind of Christian love mentioned in John 13:34, 35 might play a persuasive role in Christian relationships with people who don't believe in Jesus?

2. How do you feel about the statement, "No one comes to the Father but by me"? (John 14:6). How can such a statement be justified in a world in which a variety of paths to God is assumed as the norm?

3. When Jesus said, "I will do whatever you ask in my name" (John 14:13), how do you think He defined *whatever*? How would you interpret 15:7 in this regard?

4. Describe the kind of peace that Jesus experienced and offers to give to those who follow Him (see John 14:27; 16:33).

5. What does it mean to "remain in Jesus"? (John 15:5, 7).

6. Why do you think the Counselor (Holy Spirit) could not come until Jesus "went away"? (John 16:7).

7. Why were the disciples unable to bear everything that Jesus would have liked to say to them? (John 16:12).

Expanded Horizons

1. A. Using John 13:31–16:33, list the evidences that Jesus offers for claiming to be one with the Father.
   B. In a paragraph share the spiritual importance of Jesus' divinity to our relationship with God.

2. A. List all occurrences of the word *world* in John 14–16:33.
   B. In one or two paragraphs, indicate what you think Jesus meant by this term in this context.

When the Spirit dwells within, worship arises spontaneously.

Lesson 14

The Spirit Represents Jesus

Lesson Setting

Scripture: John 14–16.

In this lesson we pause in our progress through the Gospel of John to examine the special role of the Holy Spirit in the Gospel and in our lives today. Five crucial passages are clustered at the heart of Jesus' farewell discourse in John 14 through 16 (John 14:16, 17; 14:26; 15:26; 16:7-11; and 16:13-15). There the Spirit is called the "Comforter" or "Counselor." These "Counselor passages" need to be studied in the light of the six or seven other places in the Gospel where the Spirit is mentioned (1:32, 33; 3:5-8, 34; 4:23, 24; 6:63; 7:37-39; 20:22).

Buster was a fairly ordinary cat, but we loved him. He was no breed in particular, and his coloring was unusual; but he was a delightful combination of the two characteristics that make some cats so much fun. On the one hand, he was all cat. The mice, chipmunks, squirrels, moles, and birds in the area were all intensely aware of his presence whenever he ventured outside. The "mighty hunter" strode through his domain (ours and the neighboring yards) with an air of conscious superiority. On the other hand, when he was with children, he was as gentle and affectionate as if there were not a violent chromosome in his whole genetic makeup. His cat-play antics kept our kids amused for hours at a time. He was greatly loved by our family. And he was never gone from the house for more than twelve hours (except for the couple of times he showed up at Grandma's house a mile away—following up memories of an early-childhood "cat-sitting" experience, I suppose).

One day he disappeared. There was no trace of him for seventy-two hours. Our worries and fears increased by the hour after the first day or so. After three days the family gathered for a special prayer session. I can still hear my wife praying, "Lord, even if he is dying somewhere, please bring him back so we can know what happened. Send your angel to carry him back if You have to. We need to know what has happened to him." My wife's prayers have always been effectual.

The next morning my wife was having her devotions by the front window. She suddenly screamed out, "It's Buster! It's Buster! He's back! He's in the yard!" We all hurried out of the house in various stages of dress and undress to greet the beloved wanderer.

Describe your favorite pet to a classmate. How would you feel if someone replaced that pet with another quite like it?

He lay at the farthest corner of the yard, completely exhausted. The most obvious problem was a large hole in his side. With both sadness and joy we realized that my wife's prayers had been answered. Buster had come home to say goodbye! With broken hearts we gently carried him back into the house and called the veterinarian. But although there was an initial burst of recovery under medication, he had a massive relapse, and the family went to the veterinary clinic to say a final goodbye to our brave, beloved friend. When he saw us, he struggled to his feet to greet us and then collapsed back to the floor of his cage, barely able to breathe or open his eyes. We knew that it was over. With loud wailing and many tears, the five of us expressed our love to him one last time. We walked out of the building into sunshine, but the day seemed so dark.

When the news of Buster's death came, my wife turned immediately to the kids. "I know what we need to do. You deserve to have the joy of another animal. We need to go straight to the pet store and find a replacement for Buster."

Our teenager was mortified. "No way! No cat could ever replace Buster!"

My wife responded gently but was not deterred from her purpose. A few hours later, Snooper (the most inquisitive cat you ever saw) was exploring the house. He was as lacking in breeding as was Buster. He had tortoise-shell markings and extra-soft fur. He was just as gentle but much more disobedient. (Why should the humans have sole use of tabletops, counters, and cup-

boards?) Did he replace Buster? Yes and no. When you lose someone you love, something is always lost that can never be replaced. But in other ways, Snooper is just as special as Buster was. He fills a unique place in our hearts.

One thing would make our situation complete—to have both of them with us all the time. Maybe when Jesus comes back. . . .

Bible Search
The First Half of the Gospel
Answer the following questions on the basis of the texts provided:

1. What did the Baptist learn when he saw the Holy Spirit descend on Jesus in the form of a dove? John 1:33.
2. How important is the work of the Spirit in our lives? John 3:5.
3. How much control do human beings have over the work of the Holy Spirit? John 3:8.
4. What are the two characteristics of true worshipers? John 4:23, 24.

    Worship is not tied down to specific locations or temples, nor is it limited to any particular people. Worship does not mean coming to a particular place or even doing certain things. Worship is part of an intimate relationship with God. When the Spirit dwells within, worship arises spontaneously.
5. What is it that we receive from the Holy Spirit? John 6:63.
6. What is it that enables us to receive the Holy Spirit? John 6:63.
7. According to the Gospel of John, when

did the Holy Spirit become available? John 7:39.

Journaling
(Insight)

What practical difference does it make that the Spirit is available to everyone in every place?

Journaling
(Experience)

In what ways has the Spirit tried to make Himself known in my life recently?

The Meaning of *Comforter/Counselor*

In the Gospel of John, Jesus employs an unusual way of naming the Holy Spirit. He uses a Greek noun that can be pronounced in English as "Paraclete." This term is usually translated as *Counselor* (NIV) or *Comforter* (KJV).

The root meaning of *paraclete* is a person who is called alongside to help someone. So the word can be used in the legal sense of a defense attorney at a trial who appeals in behalf of another. As used in the Gospel of John, then, there is a strong legal connotation to the word *Counselor*, which fits well with the Spirit's role as a witness (John 15:26) who aids the disciples in their witness of Jesus.

The idea of the Spirit as a Comforter (called alongside to comfort), however, is not foreign to the farewell discourse either. The disciples would be bereft like orphans if the Spirit were not sent after Jesus' departure (14:18). The Spirit comes to help them cope with their grief at the loss of

physical contact with Jesus (16:6, 7).

Journaling
(Prayer)

Lord I need the comfort and/or counsel of the Holy Spirit in this area of my life right now. . . .

Bible Search
The Holy Spirit in John 14 through 16

Read John 14 through 16 and then answer the following questions:

8. In addition to Counselor, what other title is used for the Holy Spirit in John 14:16, 17?

9. What are two prerequisites for receiving the Holy Spirit?

10. How long is the Holy Spirit to remain with the disciples?

11. What two activities of the Holy Spirit are described in John 14:26?

    The latter part of this description is a special validation of the Gospel of John itself. The accuracy of John's memories of Jesus is assured by the ongoing presence of the Spirit with Jesus' disciples.

12. What task of the Spirit is recorded in John 15:26?

    This is a clear example of law-court language.

13. What is it that makes the coming of the Counselor possible?

14. In what three areas does the Holy Spirit bring conviction?

15. What two features of the Spirit's work are highlighted in John 16:13?

16. What does the Holy Spirit do for Jesus

according to John 16:14?

**The Role of the Holy Spirit
in the Gospel of John**

From our study of the Gospel of John, it is clear that the work of the Holy Spirit is very important. But an obsession with the Spirit is not healthy if it directs our attention away from Jesus. Jesus does not need the Holy Spirit to glorify Him in His person; the Father did that when He exalted Jesus to His right hand at the Ascension. The role

> **It is through the ever-present and available Spirit that the presence of Jesus is made real in our lives, even though we cannot see Him or touch Him.**

of the Holy Spirit is to exalt and glorify Jesus in the estimation of humanity here on earth. The Spirit is Jesus' representative or ambassador here on earth. There are no revelations from the Spirit except those that exalt and glorify Jesus. When we listen to the Holy Spirit, we are listening to Jesus Himself.

It is in this sense that the Holy Spirit can be said to represent Jesus. The Spirit is Christ's Successor and Representative, both to the disciples and to the world. The Spirit extends the presence of Jesus that the disciples experienced to the new generation who never knew the physical touch of Jesus. The teaching that Jesus could no longer do in the flesh, the Spirit would do everywhere in His behalf. The witness that He would no longer bear, the Spirit would bear in His behalf. Through the Spirit, Jesus would continue to be glorified.

On the other hand, as Jesus brought judgment and conviction to all who were exposed to His light, so the Holy Spirit has a ministry also to the world, to bring conviction of sin, the offer of righteousness, and a warning of judgment to come. The world rejected Jesus and still does so today. But in spite of the world's continued rejection, the Spirit continues to convict, and many in the second generation continue to hear Jesus' voice through the voice of the Spirit.

Above all else, it is through the ever-present and available Spirit that the presence of Jesus is made real in our lives, even though we cannot see Him or touch Him. Although others may not share our experience, those who have a relationship with Jesus can experience the supernatural guidance and comfort of the Holy Spirit.

 **Journaling**
(Experience)

I have been feeling convicted in this area of my life. . . .

 **Anchor Text**

"I have much more to say to you, more than you can now bear. But when he, the Spirit of truth, comes, he will guide you into all truth" (John 16:12, 13).

Reaction

Discussion Questions

1. Why do you think Jesus had to go away before the Spirit could convict the world of sin, righteousness, and judgment? (John 16:9-11).

2. What happens to Christians when a major spiritual leader or mentor dies or moves away? How can people go about replacing that source of spiritual strength?

3. How can people prepare for the eventual loss of some of the spiritual influences in their lives?

4. To what degree today can the Spirit help us identify true followers of God the way He helped the Baptist identify Jesus?

5. Why is it impossible to enter the kingdom of God without being born of the Spirit?

Expanded Horizons

1. With the help of a concordance, study the use of the terms *sin*, *righteousness*, and *judgment* throughout the Gospel of John.
   A. What light do the meanings of these terms shed on the Spirit's work as described in John 16:8-11?
   B. In a short paragraph, reflect on the impact each of these verses can have on devotional life today.

2. A. Make a list of all the titles and symbols that are used for the Holy Spirit in the Gospel of John (see complete listing of relevant passages in the lesson Setting).
   B. Which of these titles or symbols means the most to you in your walk with God?
   C. In a paragraph or two, share why the titles or symbols have special meaning.

Prayer should be the key of the day and the lock of the night.

Lesson 15

When Jesus Prayed for You

Lesson Setting

Scripture: John 17:1-26.

The farewell gathering of Jesus and His disciples (John 17) drew to a close with a three-part prayer. In verses 1-5 Jesus prays for Himself. In verses 6-19 His attention turns to His disciples and their need to cope with life without His physical presence. Then in verse 20, Jesus begins to speak in behalf of the second generation, those who will come to faith through the word of the disciples rather than the direct earthly ministry of Jesus.

Few who lived through it will ever forget where they were the day the Gulf War started in 1991. I was teaching a seminary class on the campus of Walla Walla College. One afternoon I was interviewing a student when Ernie Bursey, one of the religion teachers, walked by with a look of shock and dismay on his face.

"What's the matter, Ernie?" I called out as he passed by.

"Haven't you heard?" he replied. "They just started bombing Iraq."

A heavy numbness came over me as I realized that a major war had just broken out, a war whose conclusion was anything but certain at that point. People were fighting and dying, and there wasn't anything I could do about it. I finished my interviews and hurried back to the guest room so I could turn on the TV and get the details.

I was in for a shock. I knew from military analysts that in that first strike we were expected to lose more than 10 percent of our planes to Iraqi air defenses. After our bombing knocked out their airfields and their air force, the losses would diminish radically. The first wave of attackers numbered 1,700 fighters and bombers. Fully 200 expected to be shot down. Instead, all but one of the planes in the first wave came back. It was a level of military success beyond belief. No military attack in all our history had achieved such a level of success.

CNN announced that at 9:00 P.M. the Secretary of Defense and the Chairman of the Joint Chiefs of Staff would give a briefing to the nation on the aims and the results of the first attack. I fully expected them to describe a surprise attack on the airfields of Iraq. In traditional air warfare, the objective is to wipe out the opposing air force first and then to go after other targets.

> Describe a time when one of your prayers was clearly answered, either positively or negatively.

Was I in for a surprise! The newscaster reported that the airfields of Iraq weren't attacked after all! It was stated that there was only one target for the first attack (and for all the attacks after it for at least a week). That target was called "command and control." The sole purpose of the bombing was to disrupt the ability of the Iraqis to command their forces and to communicate with each other. In the Information Age, communication is the key to military success.

The Iraqi army was the fourth largest in the world. It was heavily equipped and in fairly equal numbers to the multinational coalition that stood against it. But after the destruction of its command-and-control infrastructure, it was almost helpless. During the ground war every Iraqi unit was cut off from every other. Each unit felt like it was facing the entire enemy force all by itself. Success was impossible under such conditions.

The sad reality of human warfare is that one nation's military success often means a devastating loss of life and property for the victims of war. Even the most careful "surgical strikes" result in the deaths of innocent civilians. And the political complications following a war often raise questions about the "military success."

In the New Testament, Christian life is often described in terms of warfare. So I began to think, "What is the command and control of Christian warfare? What is the key to success in the Christian's warfare with Satan?" The answer is found in John 17.

 ## Journaling
(Insight)
In what ways would seeing my life as a Christian in military terms be helpful? Be a hindrance?

 ## Journaling
(Experience)
In what ways does Christian life feel like warfare to me right now? Where is the opposition in my life right now? Or am I my own biggest enemy?

 ## Bible Search
(John 17:1-26)
Read John 17 and then answer the following questions:

1. When Jesus prays for Himself, what is His request?
2. What two benefits will result from this?
3. What is the human path to eternal life?
4. To what conviction have the disciples finally come?

    Until this point in Jesus' ministry, many or all of the disciples probably considered Jesus to be only an earthly Messiah, a glorified human being.

5. What is Jesus not praying for at this time?
6. When Jesus prays for His disciples, He does not pray that they will be removed from the world. For what does He pray?
7. Although Jesus is about to leave them, what experience does He pray the disciples will have?

8. What else does He pray they will experience?

9. For whom else does Jesus pray?

10. What does He pray will be the common experience of both the disciples and the second generation of Christians?

The remarkable thing about this chapter is the idea of Jesus praying for His disciples and for us. With all the power that Jesus displayed in the course of His ministry on earth, He still saw great value in prayer. Somehow or other, prayer accomplishes things in this world that would never happen if God's people did not pray for one another.

The Power and the Peril of Prayer for Others

After the Gulf War, the story came out about a team of three United States special forces soldiers who were airlifted 160 miles into Iraq at night to observe Iraqi movements and gain intelligence into what was going on. As morning approached they dug a foxhole, got into it, and covered it with greenery as camouflage. There they were going to sit out the day, get out at night, and then head home.

It wasn't long into that morning before one of the soldiers became curious to see what was going on out there. He lifted the camouflage just a little bit and found himself face to face with an Iraqi girl about seven years old! He knew instantly that if he pulled her into the enclosure, she would scream; so the only way to preserve the mission was to kill her on the spot and pull the

body into the foxhole. But he found himself unable to do that. So he tried in sign language to tell her not to tell her father or anybody else and let her go. But she did tell her father. In just a short time, the foxhole was surrounded by several hundred Iraqi soldiers. The bullets were flying, and heavier equipment was on its way.

But all things are possible with "command and control." The three United States soldiers radioed back to Saudi Arabia and said, "We need help. We need help NOW (160 miles away)!" A Blackhawk helicopter was sent out immediately. It flew the 160 miles in less than an hour, flying low to the ground so as to avoid radar. In fact, the Blackhawk flew so low the pilot had to do an incredible gyration to avoid a camel making its way across the desert. The helicopter arrived on the scene spraying ammunition in all directions, circled the foxhole a few times, and then came down. The three men jumped in and had a wild ride all the way back to Saudi Arabia. No one was hurt. That's the power of "command and control."

Communication is the key to modern warfare. A crucial difference between the allied coalition and Iraq was the ability to communicate when the time was right. As I reviewed the events of the Gulf War, I asked myself, "Is there a spiritual lesson here?" I believe there is.

The last great spiritual conflict on earth is called the battle of Armageddon (Revelation 16:14-16). It is not so much a military conflict as a spiritual one. Spiritual warfare does not have to do with AK-47 rifles, M1A1 tanks, and F-15 fighter-bombers. It has to do with demolishing "arguments and every pretension that sets itself up against the knowledge of God" and taking "captive every thought to make it obedient to Christ" (2 Corinthians 10:5).

Christian warfare is a battle for the mind. Have you been aware of the events in the battle for your mind this week? Do you have "control and command" over your thoughts? That's what the Christian life and Armageddon are all about. I asked myself the question, "If the Christian life involves a

Have you been aware of the events in the battle for your mind this week? Do you have "control and command" over your thoughts?

battle for the mind, if warfare is an appropriate metaphor for Christian living, then what can we learn from the Gulf War about the crucial element for spiritual victory?"

I came to the conclusion that the "command and control" of Christian warfare is nothing other than prayer. Prayer is the great communication grid that makes Christian warfare powerful and successful. I'd like to share three facts about prayer. First, it works. Second, it's dangerous. Third, it's good for us.

1. Prayer for others works. Prayer makes a big difference. I remember a time in Aus-

tralia when a pastor and his wife asked for healing. I said, "That's something I don't feel particularly gifted for, but if you really want to try, I'm willing. If you don't mind, I'd like to have the conference president with us because he's a man of God and of prayer."

We went into a back room at the church. Elder Roland Hegstad was the other speaker there, so I said, "You preach while we pray in the back; then I'll come out and do my part."

When I came out and sat on the platform, he leaned over during a song service and said, "What was going on in the back room?"

"What do you mean?"

"I have never in my life felt such a sense of the Lord's power in my preaching as in the last hour. It felt like 'radiation' coming out of the back room." I met the pastor and his wife six years later, and she had had no further trace of a potentially fatal illness. The prayers of dedicated believers had a powerful impact as I was energized by the Holy Spirit. And imagine my additional delight to discover later that at the very same time, half a world away, my wife had also been praying!

In my home church (150 members), we take time to share and pray together each Sabbath. A friend of mine, without telling anyone, was taking notes. One Sabbath he stood and asked, "Do you have any idea what's going on in this church when we pray [he's a psychologist!]? I've been keeping track for over a year, and 80 percent of the requests for prayer that we've made this year have been answered! Clinically speaking, this is overwhelming evidence. Prayer makes a difference." Prayer works!

Don't ask me why. God already knows our problems before we ask, so why should we pray about them? I don't know **why** prayer works, but I know it **does**. (I have shared only a few of many experiences here.) I am reminded of Daniel 10, where Daniel's prayers turned an entire nation around. Praying for others does make a difference.

2. Prayer is dangerous yet powerful. What do I mean by that? Keith Johnson is a Seventh-day Adventist who served in Vietnam. He tells how twelve men would go out on missions with a thirteenth man who was unarmed or lightly armed. The thirteenth one was not a medical person—he was the radio man, with plenty to carry on his back. Which man did the Viet Cong shoot at first? The one with the heaviest weapons? No, they always went for the radio man. Why? Because communication is the decisive element in a small battle as much as in a large one. The radio man can act as intelligence. He can detect enemy signals. He knows where the enemy is, how strong they are, and what kind of attack is coming. He was the key person and could turn twelve men into 12,000 on short notice. With a simple call on the radio for an airstrike by plane, helicopter, or artillery, he would give exact positions, and reinforcements would be dispatched. So, it was dangerous to carry the radio.

The Christian "command and control" element is prayer for others. Because of the power of prayer, Satan often attacks "men and women of prayer." He will do anything to keep God's people from praying. He will keep us busy with other things, but if that doesn't work, he will seek to threaten and harm. But even though people who pray place themselves at risk, the benefits of praying for others far outweigh any dangers.

Always remember, however, that God's power is greater than the enemy's. God promises to build a strong wall of protection around those who call upon Him. Yes, prayer is dangerous. But lack of prayer can be deadly!

3. Prayer for others is good for us. When we pray for people we may not like, our attitude toward them changes. It is hard to pray for someone and retain a strong dislike for that person. When we pray for people we don't naturally like, we become more like Jesus, who prayed even for His enemies.

When we pray for others, we often receive in kind. When we pray that someone will come to Christ and be forgiven, we often receive the assurance that our own sins are forgiven. When we pray for people who have hurt us, we experience forgiveness for the times we have hurt others. We are blessed. As we share the Lord's concerns for others, we develop a deeper relationship with Him.

The "How To" of Praying for Others

If you are like me, prayer has been somewhat of an up-and-down experience. Is there any way to change ingrained habits of letting prayer be the last and least part of our day? Here are a few practical suggestions.

Prayer is the key to victory in Christian warfare. Perhaps God is calling you to be a key player in His "command and control" team.

First, set aside regular time for prayer. If possible, it should be the same time every day. This helps to build a habit.

Second, make a list. Yes, I know, you may have tried that before. But sometimes you can make a prayer list too long. Your prayer list can be so long that you don't get through all the names. After a while it just seems like more work than it is worth.

Start with a short list. At the top of the list put the name of the most hopeless person you know. You know what I mean? It's the person who no matter what you do, he or she is self-destructive and impossible.

Nothing you've tried seems to help. Include the person who bugs you the most so you can learn to have the experience of praying for difficult people (no doubt you're on the top of somebody else's list—or should be!). An amazing thing happens when you pray for somebody who causes you trouble— your feelings for that person begin to change. You begin to see possibilities in that person.

Along with that difficult person, put the names of a few more promising types so that you can see results right away, because results are encouraging. Keep the list rather

Reaction

Discussion Questions

1. Why is knowing Jesus the key to eternal life? When Jesus talks about eternal life in John 17:3, is He thinking in terms of quality of life now, or is He thinking of heaven?

2. Why would Jesus avoid praying for "the world" as recorded in John 17:9?

3. What kind of unity was Jesus praying for? Is it possible to have unity of faith without unity of doctrine or belief? How wide a difference in belief can there be before disunity in relationships appears?

4. If the battle of Armageddon is primarily a spiritual event, why does the New Testament describe it in military terms?

5. Why do we often pray so little for people we don't naturally like?

Expanded Horizons

1. Think of Jesus' prayer in John 17 as a "report" of His activities here on earth to the "command center." Write out His "report" in your own words, giving particular emphasis to the things Jesus has done to carry out His orders. Include also the results of Jesus' activities.

short. As the Holy Spirit impresses you, take someone off the list and add another.

Third, ask a friend to keep you accountable, someone to help you follow through on your resolutions and promises. The best person to ask may be what I call a hard-nosed friend. A hard-nosed friend is a person who knows you've promised to spend from 7:00–7:15 A.M. daily in prayer. You invite that friend to hold you accountable. The next morning at 7:17 the phone rings. It's your friend. He or she says, "Did you?" A hard-nosed friend is the kind of friend who will tell you what you need to hear even when you really don't want to hear it.

 ## Journaling
(Prayer)

Help me find the accountability I need to become more consistent in prayer.

Help me to sense who among my friends and family is most in need of my prayers right now.

 ## Anchor Text

"My prayer is not for them alone. I pray also for those who will believe in me through their message" (John 17:20).

133

2. A. The following passages (among others) in the Gospel of John use the word *glory*—a central theme of John 17—1:14; 2:11; 7:18; 8:50; 12:23, 24; 12:41; 14:13; 15:8; 17:10; 21:19. (Hint: in some texts the translators substitute words such as *honor*.) Summarize in a sentence for each of these texts what it says about glory.

B. Summarize the main themes of these texts in a short paragraph.

C. In a paragraph reflect on how we can glorify God in our lives today.

"May I never boast except in the cross of our Lord Jesus Christ."

Lesson 16

The Cross: What's the Big Deal?

Lesson Setting

Scripture: John 18:1–19:42.

The story of Jesus' crucifixion in the Gospel of John begins and ends in a garden (18:1; 19:41) and falls naturally into three parts. First, there is a section describing the betrayal, arrest, and indictment of Jesus (18:1-27). The central section is concerned with the trial before Pilate (18:28–19:16). The crucifixion and burial of Jesus are described in 19:16-42.

With a heavy heart John followed Jesus down the stairs leading from the upper room. Jesus had just celebrated the Passover with His disciples, minus Judas. Judas had left the room hours before and, for some reason, did not return. That was just it. Jesus had dropped some dark hints of betrayal in the disciples' ears and left the impression that Judas was the one He was talking about. But that was impossible! Judas had always been the steady, sensible one! Did Jesus really know something, or was He just being suspicious? It did seem strange, though, that Judas hadn't returned. Where had he gone?

John's thoughts were interrupted by the awareness that the group had reached the long public staircase that wound down from Mount Zion toward the Ophel Ridge, just south of the temple. For a while John concentrated on the placement of his feet, working his way one step at a time. *Not the greatest piece of work,* he grumbled to himself as he noticed anew the unevenness of the steps.

Night had fallen, but it was still early. The stair-step street was largely dark, but the occasional house torch supplemented the light of the torches Peter and Nathanael had thought to bring along. John pulled his cloak tighter as he sensed the chill air of a March evening at Jerusalem's elevation. Every so often a gap in the buildings to the left allowed a glimpse of the brightly lighted temple, looking ever larger and more imposing as they worked their way eastward down the hill. When buildings blocked a view of the temple, they were silhouetted against the golden glow of the night sky over the temple. John found himself unable to get excited about the festivities that would take

Has any personal friend or relative ever made a major sacrifice in your behalf? How did that make you feel about that person? About yourself?

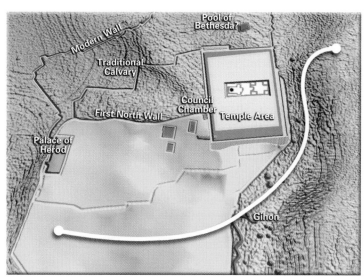

Jesus' route from the upper room to the Garden of Gethsemane

place up there the next day.

Soon they reached the bottom of Mount Zion and went up the small rise to the top of Ophel Ridge. To the left was the giant marble staircase that Jesus and the disciples had used many times to enter the temple courtyard. But tonight Jesus showed no interest in the temple; He was heading elsewhere. Soon they went out the Water Gate and down the steep, winding path from the Ophel Ridge to the Kidron Valley.

From there they headed north up the valley until the temple was once more above and to the left, while in front of them and to the right was the Mount of Olives, glowing duskily in the spillover of light from the temple mount. Walking around Jerusalem was a great way to stay in shape! Somehow John's legs seemed more tired than usual.

It looked as if Jesus was planning to spend some prayer time in the Garden of Gethsemane again. John wondered what was on Jesus' mind this time. What had Jesus meant when He said He was about to leave them? Did it really have something to do with betrayal and death as He had suggested so often? John's thoughts were turning as dark as the Valley of Kidron in midevening.

When they arrived at the garden, Jesus left eight of the disciples at the entrance as if to guard the place. He took John, Peter, and James with Him and left them together while He went even farther into the garden to pray. John tried to pray, but his mind wandered almost immediately, and he realized how tired he was. *Let me get comfortable on this patch of grass,* John thought. *I'll just rest my eyes for a couple of minutes, and then my mind will concentrate better on God.*

John awakened with a jolt, realizing that he had been deeply asleep for some time. For a minute he was disoriented. As his mind slowly came back to reality, it hit him: *That's Judas's voice! He finally found us! Great! The team is back together again. . . .*

Bible Search
(John 18:1-27)

Three major events are portrayed in John 18:1-27: Jesus' arrest in the garden (1-11), His interrogation before Annas, the father-in-law of Caiaphas, the high priest (12-14, 19-24), and Peter's three denials of Jesus (15-18, 25-27). The latter two events intertwine in a movement between the courtyard, where Peter is, and the interrogation chamber, where Jesus is.

Read John 18:1-27 and answer the following questions:

1. When Jesus leaves the upper room with His disciples, where does He lead them?

2. How was Judas, with the detachment of soldiers, able to find Jesus?

3. Was Jesus surprised that Judas found Him? Explain your answer.

4. What happened when Jesus announced to the mob who He was?

5. What request did Jesus make?

6. How did Jesus respond to Peter's courageous attempt to defend Him?

7. Why did one of the officials strike Jesus in the face?

8. How did Peter get into the high priest's courtyard?

9. Under what circumstances was Peter asked if he was one of Jesus' disciples?

10. Who recognized Peter by the fire?

The very boldness of Peter in the garden makes him a target here.

In John 18:1-11 the main point seems to be that Jesus is in full control of the situation, in fulfillment of John 10:18: " 'No one takes my life from me, but I lay it down of my own accord.' " Although He is about to be murdered, Jesus is not a victim in John's Gospel; He is in control of events. For example, if Jesus had wanted to avoid arrest, He could have simply gone somewhere other than the garden, where Judas would know to look for Him. He leads His disciples to the garden, even though He knows what will happen there. He suffers no anguish in John's account; He is in full control of His emotions. He does not wait for the mob to come to Him; He moves forward and addresses them, showing the ability to fully

intimidate them if that would have served His purpose. His death is voluntary. They could not have arrested Him had He not allowed it. And He gains the release of His disciples as well.

Under the circumstances, the reaction of Peter is almost amusing. Although Jesus is fully in control of the situation, Peter sees things as totally out of control; so he flashes his sword and becomes a slasher for Jesus. But Jesus tells him to put his sword away. Peter's good intentions would prevent events from unfolding the way God had planned. Jesus must go to the cross, or God's plan of salvation would fail. Peter does not know this. His actions to gain control of the situation would only have moved things truly out of control.

Journaling
(Insight)

What difference does it make that no situation is beyond Jesus' ability to control? To what degree can Jesus' ability be applied to my life today?

Journaling
(Experience)

What area(s) of my life seem out of control right now? How can confidence in Jesus' lordship over my life help me deal with my fears?

Journaling
(Prayer)

Thank You for the assurance that everything that happens to me is important to You. Give me confidence in You to face all of life without fear. Help me to feel that even when bad things happen to me, You can bring good out of it.

Jesus is quite assertive in His encounter with Annas (John 18:20-23). He challenges both the secretiveness of His arrest ("I said nothing in secret") and the legal procedure being followed ("Why question me?"). He even tosses in a dash of humor ("If I spoke the truth, why did you strike me?"). He certainly does not follow an extreme interpretation of His own statement about turning the other cheek (Matthew 5:39). He protests His opponent's abuse of authority. Evidently, being like Jesus is not the same as being a doormat. It is appropriate for Christians to set boundaries in their relationships with others. Allowing other people to walk all over us generally helps no one. There is sometimes a fine line between being humble and being abused.

Journaling
(Insight)
I don't have to become a "wimp" in order to be like Jesus.

Only in the Gospel of John do we become aware that more than one disciple followed Jesus into the high priest's courtyard. Presumably, the girl at the door knew that John ("another disciple") was a disciple of Jesus but chose not to challenge His entrance. Peter was not so lucky. Peter had come boldly to the front at the time of Jesus' arrest. Now that boldness challenges him to further boldness, but he fails the test. Poor impulsive Peter. Too bold one minute, too timid the next!

Bible Search
Trial Before Pilate
Read John 18:28–19:16 and answer the following questions:

11. When Jesus was led to the palace of the Roman governor the next morning, why did the Jewish leaders stay outside?
12. Why did the Jews bring Jesus to Pilate?
13. What accusations had the Jews brought against Jesus?
     This would make Him a threat to Caesar.
14. What argument did Jesus make to show Pilate that he didn't need to be concerned about the accusation?
15. What kind of king is Jesus?
16. How do we know Pilate was convinced by Jesus' argument?
17. When the religious leaders refused to accept Pilate's decision, what did he decide to do to Jesus?
18. What new charge did the Jewish leaders bring against Jesus?
19. Did Pilate change his mind about Jesus at that point?
20. What shocking statement did the desperate Jewish leaders make?

Pilate is the central figure of this part of the narrative. Historically, he was in a position of considerable political weakness. A series of blunders had repeatedly offended the religious sensibilities of the Jews. He was, therefore, unpopular with the Jews, and his fitness to rule had even come under suspicion in the palace of the emperor in Rome. One more major conflict with the religious leaders, and he would be out of office. This made him extremely vulnerable to blackmail.

In approaching Pilate, the priests formulate their charge against Jesus in the political terms that a Roman governor could appreciate. Jesus must be executed because his kingship is a threat to Caesar. But Jesus' statement, "My kingdom is not of this world," makes it clear to Pilate that Jesus' claim to kingship is no political or military threat to Rome. Pilate determines to free Jesus but at the same time provides the Jewish leaders a face-saving way out, offering to release Jesus on the basis of a traditional prisoner release rather than a judgment of innocence.

Things get complicated for Pilate when the Jewish leaders reject his offer. They want Jesus dead at any cost. That means that Pilate must either persuade them against their set opinion or release Jesus in the face of their wrath, which he cannot afford to do politically. So he is forced into a dilemma between justice and self-interest.

Pilate seeks, therefore, to excite the religious leaders' sympathy by flogging Jesus and presenting Him before them. But they refuse to be moved. Sensing that Pilate's self-interest has weakened him, the religious leaders start playing dirty; they argue that Jesus should die because He has broken their religious law. Pilate cannot afford to be seen as allowing sacrilege against the Jewish religion.

Pilate now realizes that his indecision has been his weakness. He cannot save both himself and Jesus. He determines to save himself and then some. He will consent to the religious leaders' request, but they will pay dearly for it. He condemns Jesus in exchange for a public confession of their obligation to serve Caesar, "We have no king but Caesar."

Earlier Caiaphas had insisted that one Man had to be sacrificed so that the nation might not be destroyed (11:48-52). Now he is ready to sacrifice the nation in order to destroy one Man. The religious leaders reject Jesus' kingship with such passion that they now rejoice in a king whom they have always hated. Pilate intends to hold them to that pledge in the future. They will have no more power over him. From this point on in the Gospel story, Pilate is unmovable. The death of Jesus makes him strong.

Journaling
(Experience)

Are there areas of life where I have become vulnerable to spiritual blackmail because of sin or expediency?

Journaling
(Insight)

How easily people do what they know to be wrong when self-interest gets in the way.

Bible Search
The Crucifixion Itself

Crucifixion was a peculiarly Roman form of execution. Some people were nailed; others were tied with ropes. The key element, however, was that in order to breathe, victims had to push up with their feet to raise their bodies somewhat. Death came by suffocation when they became too weary to raise themselves anymore. Death was, therefore, slow and painful. Breaking the legs, of course, would hasten the process, when that was for the executioners' convenience. An additional element of torture was shame and exposure, being hung naked in front of family and friends.

Read John 19:16-42 and answer the following questions:

21. What inscription did Pilate cause to be

placed on the cross of Jesus?

22. How did Pilate respond to the chief priests' attempt to soften the implications of the inscription?

23. What major theme of this passage occurs four times?

24. What were Jesus' last words?

25. What two individuals took care of the body of Jesus and provided the tomb?

In verses 19-22 the "new" Pilate strikes again. The wording he chose for the inscription placed on the cross made the crucifixion of Jesus symbolic of Rome's dominance over Palestine and Judaism. With the inscription he turned the crucifixion into a public spectacle designed as a blow to the prestige of the Jews and their religious leaders. Although Pilate feels in control of matters, God is the One in control. Jesus' death is voluntary, purposeful, and according to the Scriptures.

The Cross—What's the Big Deal?

When Jesus pronounced the words "It is finished" (John 19:30) on the cross, what exactly was finished? What makes the Cross so special that Paul would refuse to glory in anything else? (Galatians 6:14).

The particular emphasis in the Gospel of John seems to be that the Cross is the fulfillment of the Bible prophecies pointing toward the Messiah. Prophecy was fulfilled right down to the minutest detail of just what type of garment was divided, what type was wagered for (23, 24), and just how the body of Jesus was handled after His death (35-37). The Cross makes it clear that God has foreseen it all ahead of time and is in full control of the situation.

The law of God was also fulfilled on the Cross. God was never more faithful to His covenant than He was when He dealt out the wages of sin (Romans 6:23) to Jesus as the representative of the sinful human race. If the law of God could have been changed, humanity could have been saved without a Cross. It is the Cross that makes it possible to save the human race while at the same time preserving the peace and the order of the universe (2 Corinthians 5:14, 15). The Cross condemns human sin in the person of Christ (Romans 8:3; 1 Peter 2:24); the Resurrection affirms the whole human race because of the perfect life of Jesus (Acts 13:32, 33; 2 Corinthians 5:21).

Above all else, the Cross affirms the value of each person. God so loves every person that Jesus would have died for even one. As a full-fledged member of the Godhead and as the Creator of the universe, Jesus possesses infinite value in His person. In dying for you and me, Jesus testified to the infinite value He places on every one of us. You and I are worth everything to Him. And the value that we have in the Cross is a value that does not change, no matter what we do or who we become. We may be the poorest of the poor, yet our value is infinite in the Cross. We may fail a hundred times, yet our value is infinite in the Cross. We may be despised and rejected by everyone we meet, yet our value is infinite in the Cross. And

We may fail a hundred times, yet our value is infinite in the Cross.

that value is set for eternity. If we should, in the end, choose to reject the Cross, our value in eternity will be measured by the pain of our absence that is felt in the heart of God.

When we gain a sense of our value in the Cross, we can begin to avoid the ups and downs that come when our self-worth is based on performance or on the fickle opinions of others. When we see ourselves in the light of the Cross, the Holy Spirit provides strength to overcome sin, the confidence to defeat Satan, and the joy that comes from knowing who we are. No wonder Paul said, "May I never boast except in the Cross of our Lord Jesus Christ" (Galatians 6:14).

 **Journaling**
(Insight)

Journal about the aspect of the Cross that has meant the most to you.

 **Journaling**
(Prayer)

Pray that the meaning of the Cross will become more plain and be the motivating center of your life.

 **Anchor Text**

"Jesus said, 'My kingdom is not of this world. If it were, my servants would fight to prevent my arrest by the Jews. But now my kingdom is from another place'" (John 18:36).

Reaction

Discussion Questions

1. How do you think Jesus was able to overcome the natural human instinct toward self-preservation when He led the disciples to the garden, knowing that Judas was likely to lead His enemies there?

2. Does Jesus' assertiveness make you uncomfortable? Why? If you were to meet the Jesus described in this Gospel, would you naturally like Him or dislike Him? Why?

3. How could Peter be so brave one minute and so wimpy an hour or two later? How were the two situations different?

4. What is the difference between assertiveness and aggressiveness? Can they be easily mistaken for one another?

5. If you had been present at the trial of Jesus, what would you have done? Kept silent? Protested verbally? Joined in when people abused Jesus? What would be the primary motivation for your actions?

6. What kinds of strategies can help one avoid the character weaknesses that placed Pilate in conflict with his own conscience?

Expanded Horizons

1. There are several key individuals in the narrative of John 18 and 19: Jesus, Judas, Peter, Annas, and Pilate.
   A. Describe the mental and emotional state of each of them with one or two words.
   B. Write a short paragraph in which you describe how you think their emotions affected their actions in the narrative.

2. Note the various times that Pilate addresses Jesus during the trial. Write a brief explanation of why you think Jesus responds on some occasions but remains silent on others.

3. Design a logo that will express the meaning that the Cross has for you personally.

Because Jesus rose from the dead, no other miracle is impossible.

Lesson 17

The Power of the Resurrection

Lesson Setting

Scripture: John 20:1-31.

With John 20 we have arrived at a crucial point in the Gospel of John. Jesus has had His farewell meeting with the disciples in chapters 13 through 17, and He has suffered His trial and death in chapters 18 and 19. There is a sense in which the story is "finished" with Jesus' death on the cross (see 19:30).

But there is also a sense in which it is unfinished. There would be no Christian church if Jesus had remained in the tomb. His resurrection truly let the disciples know that the gospel is good news. Chapter 20 reports Jesus' all-important resurrection and His appearances to His disciples.

145

I still can't believe it," Thomas moaned to his wife in the motel room. "This should never have happened."

"Why didn't you *do* something, instead of running away?"

"Did you have to bring that up again? It's embarrassing enough for everybody to know that I spent three years of my life following someone who turned out to be a fraud. I just couldn't bear watching Him be crucified," Thomas said for perhaps the twentieth time.

"But He *needed* you," his wife shot back. "I saw Him looking around in that crowd for a friendly face, for someone—anyone—who cared. Were any of the Twelve there? No."

"There you go exaggerating again. You yourself said that John went right past the soldiers to the foot of Jesus' cross." Thomas's sorrow was turning to anger.

"Yes, John **did** come up to the foot of the cross for a couple of minutes, but that was

only because Jesus' mother made him take her. You could see on his face that he really wanted to be someplace else, **anyplace** else.

"So, what did **you** do, brave woman?"

"I tried to press as close as I could without getting in the way of the soldiers, but Jesus hardly knew me," she retorted. "What could I have said that would have helped Him, anyway? I've never been a great talker."

"You're gabbing just fine right now." Thomas put his hands over his ears and moved to the door. "I've got to get outside for some fresh air."

"Running away again!" she stated emphatically as she followed him part-way out the door.

Thomas strode away from the motel and his female "conscience." It was a sunny Monday afternoon, just three days after Jesus had died and been buried. Rumors abounded about strange happenings at the tomb of

Recall a time when something totally unexpected and absolutely delightful happened to you. How did your feelings change from just before the happening to right afterward? How did that surprise change your life?

JOHNs-10

Jesus yesterday, but Thomas wouldn't listen to any of it. In his saner moments, he was toying with returning to Galilee and looking for a job in the fishing industry. People always had to eat.

He hadn't gone a hundred yards when he saw John coming. John had been impossible to live with since Friday. The closest one to Jesus at the Last Supper on Thursday. The only one at the cross. The first one at the tomb. The one Jesus said He loved the most. You'd think Jesus' death was a blessing the way John talked. He was the last person Thomas wanted to see just then, but what's the use in being rude when you're running out of friends and even your wife is disappointed in you? John looked especially excited this time.

"Thomas! I'm glad I found you here. You're not going to believe this, Thomas! We saw Him! We saw Him last night. He came right into the room where we had that last supper with Him. He said, 'Peace be with you.' I had my doubts at first, but then He showed us the nail marks in His hand and the wound in His side. It was Him! He's alive!"

John was out of control as usual. Thomas's expression barely changed. Nothing surprised him anymore.

"Get a grip on yourself, John," Thomas said evenly. "You've been telling stories all weekend. I really don't have time for this."

"But this is real," John replied earnestly, trying to tone down his enthusiasm for Thomas's sake. "I saw Him, I heard Him, He ate something in front of us."

"But did you *touch* Him?" Thomas retorted.

"Why would I do that? You just don't go putting your hands all over the Master!"

"Listen to me, John. Unless I see with my own eyes the nail marks in his hands and put my finger where the nails were and put my hand into His side, I will not believe it. . . ."

Bible Search
(John 20:1-31)

Read John 20:1-31 and then answer the following questions:

1. When Mary Magdalene arrived at the tomb of Jesus, what did she see?
2. After Mary had notified the disciples, Peter and John ran for the tomb. Which one arrived outside the tomb first? Which one entered the tomb first? Which was the first one to believe that Jesus was raised from the dead?
3. How much of the study of the Scriptures had prepared the disciples for the resurrection of Jesus from the dead?
4. What did Mary Magdalene think had happened to Jesus' body?
5. How did Mary come to realize that Jesus was alive?

   To the second generation of Christians, the message in this little scene was powerful. Although Mary was in the personal presence of Jesus, her eyes were so blinded by tears that she had no idea who He was. His physical presence was of no use to her until she gave attention to His word. We, too, have that word, through the Gospel of John.

6. How did the rest of the disciples come to know that Jesus was raised from the dead?

146

7. How did Thomas come to know that Jesus was raised from the dead?

 Journaling
(Insight)

If even the disciples of Jesus had difficulty believing, should I get down on myself when I struggle for faith or when I fail?

 Journaling
(Experience)

In what ways have I had a decisive and life-changing encounter(s) with Jesus?

 Journaling
(Prayer)

Help me know how to "touch" Your hands and side today.

The Resurrection and Appearances of Jesus

According to the Life Application Bible, the New Testament records a total of eleven separate post-resurrection appearances of Jesus. Jesus appeared to Mary Magdalene by herself (Mark 16:9-11; John 20:10-18) and possibly on another occasion in the company of other women (Matthew 28:8-10). He appeared to Peter by himself in Jerusalem (Luke 24:34; 1 Corinthians 15:5) and to two travelers on the road to Emmaus (Luke 24:13-35; Mark 16:12, 13).

Jesus appeared to the disciples behind locked doors (Mark 16:14; Luke 24:36-43; John 20:19-25) and then to the same group with the addition of Thomas (John 20:24-29; 1 Corinthians 15:5). He appeared to seven disciples while they were fishing in Galilee (John 21:1-23) and to eleven disciples on a mountain (Matthew 28:16-20). Finally, He appeared to those who watched Him ascend into heaven (Luke 24:44-49; Acts 1:3-11). In addition to these narrative accounts, Paul asserts that Jesus also appeared privately to His brother James (1 Corinthians 15:7) and publicly to a crowd of 500 (verse 6).

The many witnesses to the resurrection provided a safeguard against the accusation that accounts of the resurrection were the fabrication of a handful of disappointed disciples, trying to save face. As long as these disciples lived, their stories could be compared and checked out (Luke 1:1-4). The author of the Fourth Gospel was the last living disciple who had witnessed the resurrection of Jesus.

But perhaps the greatest evidence of Jesus' resurrection, especially for the second generation, who had no living witness to the event, was the fact of the empty tomb. Since the risen Jesus was able to pass through solid objects (note verses 19 and 26 in the same chapter), the entrance stone was not rolled away so that Jesus could get out of the tomb but to let the disciples get in and verify that the tomb was now empty. Given the circumstances, the emptiness of the tomb is extremely hard to understand unless Jesus was, in fact, raised from the dead. How did the tomb become empty? Certainly the enemies of Jesus had no motive for removing His body from the tomb; and if they had done so, why didn't they just produce the body to prove that He had not risen?

It is equally clear that the disciples had

neither the ability nor the intention of stealing Jesus' body (it is the chief priests who raise the possibility—Matthew 27:62-64). While Jesus was still alive, they showed an abysmal lack of courage (Matthew 26:56; Mark 14:50; John 18:17, 25-27), so why would their courage increase after His death? The fact is that the disciples did not believe that Jesus would allow Himself to die, in spite of His repeated assertions of what lay ahead (Mark 8:31-33; 9:30-32; 10:32-34). They were very slow to believe His resurrection, when, in fact, He proved to be alive again (John 20:1-9, 24-29). In any case, the

Who would suffer ridicule, torture, and death over an event that never took place?

guard of Roman soldiers provided formidable evidence that no such act was committed (Matthew 27:62-64; 28:11-15). If the disciples had stolen the body of Jesus, their later behavior is totally unexplainable. Who would sacrifice fame, fortune, and family to spread a hoax throughout the world? Who would suffer ridicule, torture, and death over an event that never took place?

If neither the disciples of Jesus nor His enemies stole His body, the empty tomb conclusively demonstrates the reality of Jesus' resurrection. And if Jesus rose from the dead, the implications for today are enormous. For one thing, if Jesus rose from the dead, no other miracle is impossible or incredible. Anything the second generation

could possibly ask of Him can be done if it is according to His will. Our own resurrection is guaranteed by the certainty of His. Not only so, the same divine power that raised Jesus from the dead can bring life and healing into even the most hopeless human situations.

 **Journaling**
(Insight)

The basis of Christian faith is founded on solid history (the empty tomb).

The Power of His Resurrection

"I want to know the power of His resurrection," Paul wrote to the Philippians (3:10). The resurrection of Jesus was the most awesome event of all time. With all of our advances in science and technology, we still have no clue how to bring the dead back to life. Anyone who has the power to raise the dead has the power to accomplish anything else that the human race might need.

At the heart of Christian faith is the testimony of the New Testament that Jesus rose from the dead. It describes that action as an act of God on the same scale as the original creation. The power of the resurrection becomes the basis for the mighty acts of God in the lives of Christians ever since (2 Corinthians 5:14-17). The power of the resurrection is the basis for limitless power in the lives of Christians today.

Why, then, are these "limitless powers" so invisible in many churches? Why is it so hard to see the mighty hand of God in a secular world? It is simply because we often forget to put Him first in our lives. The secret of powerful living is found in a regular practice of the Old Testament saints.

Bible Search

Answer the following questions on the basis of the texts provided:

8. What is the appropriate response when God does "wonders" in your life? Psalm 105:5.

9. Read Psalm 78:1-12. List five actions that can help us obey God.

One of the major themes of the Old Testament has to do with remembering and forgetting. Whenever the Israelites forgot the mighty things God had done for them, they lost the power of the faith and the sense of His living presence. When they remembered what He had done for them in the past, the power of the original action was reactivated in their lives. In fact, the very essence of Old Testament spiritual life was recounting the mighty acts of God in their past history. And it was no empty retelling. When the Israelites told of the mighty acts of God in their past history, the power of the original act was unleashed again in their experience.

What was true in Old Testament times was also true of the New Testament. The greatest intervention of God was at the Cross and the resurrection of Jesus. The secret of Christian power is the constant retelling of the Christ event. To talk about Jesus is no empty retelling. The power of the Resurrection is unleashed in the life of anyone who tells others about what Christ has done for him or her.

That is why sharing our faith is such an essential part of the Christian experience. Where there is no retelling of the mighty acts of God, there is no power. But telling what God has done brings revival and reformation into the church. The power of the Resurrection turns a formal religion into a living and powerful one!

Real Christianity is filled with awesome power and excitement. Don't settle for less.

The antidote to boring, lifeless religion is to become part of the living and active power of God by remembering and retelling what God has done: what God did in Old Testament times, what God did at the Cross, and what God has done and is doing in the personal experience of each one of us. Real Christianity is filled with awesome power and excitement. Don't settle for less.

Journaling
(Prayer)

Make the power of the Resurrection real in my life today.

Journaling
(Experience)

In what ways have I recounted Your mighty acts, Lord? How can I make this more a part of my life?

Anchor Text

"Thomas said to him, 'My Lord and my God!' " (John 20:28).

Reaction

1. Are there times when it is good to be as skeptical as Thomas was? How do we know when it is appropriate to doubt something?

2. What are some of the things in life that blind us to the presence and the power of Jesus? How can we learn to see Him in the everyday experiences of life?

3. According to John 20:9, when the disciples searched the Scriptures after the crucifixion, they found no evidence that Jesus would be raised from the dead. How should we respond when we fail to find answers to our questions in the Bible?

4. If you had been a disciple of Jesus at the time, what would you have said to try to convince Thomas?

5. Which argument for the resurrection of Jesus do you think would be the most impressive to the typical unbeliever today?

6. Why is it so easy to forget the great things that God has done in your life?

Expanded Horizons

Use the specific references on the handout "Reflection on the Resurrection of Jesus" provided by your teacher to learn more about the post-resurrection appearances of Jesus to His disciples and others.

Lord of second chances, here I am again!

Lesson 18

The Greatest Comeback in History

Lesson Setting

Scripture: John 21:1-25.

John 21 is often described as the Epilogue to the Fourth Gospel because it comes after what sounds like the concluding words of the Gospel in 20:30, 31. It tells the story of how the disciples encountered Jesus in Galilee after His resurrection. Jesus helps them find a huge catch of fish (1-6), fixes breakfast (7-14), and then holds a serious conversation on the beach with Peter (15-23).

The impression one gets, particularly in the Gospel of John, is that Jesus' post-resurrection appearances were occasional and rather unexpected. Mary, the ten, Thomas, and now seven disciples are all startled at the suddenness of Jesus' appearances to them. In a real sense, the ministry of Jesus to His disciples was completed in the upper room (John 13–17). He says very little to them after the Resurrection. The purpose of His appearances is to validate the reality of His resurrection.

I'm going fishing," Peter said. "I'm tired of waiting around, trying to figure out what to do, wondering if and when Jesus is going to show up next." He half-expected the others to reject his suggestion out of hand. They were reluctant to go back on their decision to leave fishing and follow Jesus. But this time the others were on the same wavelength as Peter.

"We'll go with you," they replied and got the boat ready for departure.

It was almost as if some sort of curse was upon them. The boat went out, the sun went down, the lake became pitch dark, and still they didn't catch any fish. You see, people fished at night in Galilee because they used nets. With lure fishing you dangle something attractive in front of the fish in daylight and hope it decides to have a bite (in which case you get to have a bite). But if you tried net fishing during the day, the fish would see the net coming and swim away. So you fish at night and hope your net runs into a school of big ones by surprise. This time Peter and the other disciples fished all night and caught nothing.

Peter alternated between brooding over his failure a few weeks before (when he denied Jesus in the high priest's courtyard) and lots of loud talking to keep everyone awake and his own inner fears at bay. It was great that Jesus was alive again. But things were different now. It seemed harder to get close to Him anymore. How Peter wished He could have had a chance to talk to Jesus one on one, explain what had happened in the high priest's courtyard, and tell Jesus how sorry he was. Now it had been weeks since Jesus had made an appearance. Might as well go fishing. The waiting around was driving Peter nuts. What if he never got to make things right? Never got to find out how Jesus felt about him?

Recall a time when your parents caught you doing something very different from what you were supposed to be doing. What were your feelings at that moment? How did the situation work itself out?

Morning came. The sun was just about to break over the mountains to the east. "Guess we're down to one last chance," Peter said to no one in particular. Immediately a couple of the disciples grabbed the pull ropes and pulled the net around to the port side of the boat. You see, when the sun broke out over the hills to the east in the morning, there was one final opportunity to surprise the fish. If you placed the nets in the shadow of the boat, you just might catch a few sleepy fish trying to get their eyes adjusted to the bright light, wandering into the shadow of the boat! *After a night like this, it's always worth a shot,* Peter thought to himself.

Suddenly there was a stranger standing on the shore. No one thought they had ever seen Him before. He called out, "Throw your net on the right side (starboard) of the boat." The disciples looked at each other and then looked at Peter. Whatever this man's profession was, He knew nothing about fishing! Then Peter spoke, "Do what the man said! Nothing else has worked; we might as well try."

A minute or so after the net was in place, the entire boat jerked around suddenly. Peter grabbed for the railing to steady himself and focused his eyes on the net. It was being shoved this way and that by some of the biggest fish Peter had ever seen! Loads of them! Every so often the struggling mass seemed to find a sense of purpose and dart off in some direction, only to be stopped by the net, at the expense of another huge jerk on the boat.

"Hey, guys!" John said excitedly, looking toward the shore, "It's the Lord!"

Peter's head snapped around and gazed intently toward the shore. John's eyes were younger, but he'd know that grin anywhere. Peter's face set with determination. *I'm not going to miss this chance! We need to talk!* Peter thought to himself.

"Take over, guys. I'm going in," Peter yelled.

"What?" said Nathanael with amazement as Peter dove right out of the boat into the lake and began pounding the water with powerful strokes.

At last, Peter thought. *It's time to put this behind me. . . .*

Journaling
(Experience)

If Jesus tried to contact me in the course of my everyday life, would I recognize Him? Would I even be open to such contact? Why?

Journaling
(Prayer)

Lord, help me be more aware of Your hand in my life and in the lives of those around me.

Bible Search
(John 21:1-25)

Read John 21:1-25 and then answer the following questions:

1. How many disciples decide to go out fishing with Peter? Compare with Matthew 10:2 and Mark 3:17.
2. Which unnamed disciple was part of this group?
3. How did they succeed in catching fish?
4. Who first recognized that it was Jesus standing on the shore? What did Peter

do when he finally recognized Jesus on the shore?

5. What had Jesus been doing on the shore?

6. In this chapter is a threefold conversation between Jesus and Peter (vs. 15, 16, 17). On a sheet of paper make four columns with the following headings.

John 21	Jesus Asks	Peter Replies	Jesus Responds
v. 15			
v. 16			
v. 17			

For each verse put the exact words of the conversation between Jesus and Peter under the appropriate heading.

7. How does Peter feel about this three-fold exchange?

8. What other concern does Peter have?

9. How does the Gospel end?

 **Journaling**

(Insight)

Is Jesus often the agent behind events that hurt people's feelings, or would Peter have felt hurt no matter what Jesus said or did? What implications are there for my feelings and how I deal with them?

In the fishing story of John 21, Jesus acted here as the second Adam. The original Adam, according to Genesis 1:26-28, was told to "rule over the fish of the sea." Jesus here demonstrated His ability to rule over the fish of the sea. The 153 fish represented the second generation of believers, those who came to faith because of the direct efforts of the disciples, but under the oversight of Jesus Himself.

It appears that breakfast was pretty silent. The disciples didn't seem to know what to make of Jesus' behavior since they had been with Him in the upper room. In a real sense, they shared here the same uncertainties that the second generation of Christians would experience over the death of the beloved disciple. The coming of the Spirit would provide solid assurance, and that reality proved to be the same for both the first and second generation.

Getting Peter Back on Track

After breakfast, Peter and Jesus have a long-awaited conversation. Jesus questions Peter three times about the depth and sincerity of their relationship, no doubt in intentional response to Peter's three denials of Jesus described in John 18:15-18, 25-27. The first time Jesus adds a phrase, "Do you truly love me *more than these*?" (emphasis supplied). Does Peter love Jesus more than the other disciples do? Jesus needed to draw Peter out on this point because he had been so quick earlier to boast that his loyalty exceeded that of the others (Matthew 26:33). But when Peter refuses to respond to that part of the question, Jesus accepts his silence as confession and does not press the point further. What counts is the depth of your relationship with Jesus, not how well that depth compares with others.

Verses 15-17 describe a threefold repetition of question, reply, and response. This is unexpected and could even seem rude on the part of Jesus. The effect is to probe Peter to the depths of his being, at the cost of considerable pain. After his denial when he went out weeping, he lost that bravado (Peter's self-confidence and assertiveness are gradually chipped away), until he is left with nothing but the certainty that Jesus knows his heart and will be fair in His judgments.

"No pain, no gain" seems to be a law of spiritual growth. Those who have advanced far in spiritual life are usually those who

Jesus doesn't settle for quick, superficial answers. He insists on getting down to the true feelings and motives of those He loves.

have suffered much. There is something about pain, loss, poverty, and emotional anguish that can bring people to the place where major gains in spiritual development are possible. And sometimes, as happened in the case of Peter, the author of that pain is Jesus Himself, who, like a loving surgeon, wounds so that He might heal. Jesus doesn't settle for quick, superficial answers. He insists on getting down to the true feelings and motives of those He loves. The process, however, usually demands a price.

In the text, the threefold dialogue seems to take place in the presence of the other disciples at the breakfast location. But verse 20 implies that Jesus and Peter are walking alone along the beach. Ellen G. White suggests that between the events of verses 17 and 18, Jesus and Peter got up and began

their private conversation as they walked along (*The Desire of Ages*, 815). If so, the conversation recorded in verses 15-17 happened in front of the other disciples. Peter's confession was not for his sake alone. The other disciples needed to regain confidence in Peter after his terrible betrayal of Jesus in the high priest's courtyard. Public sin needs to be publicly confessed in order to get a truly fresh start in life.

In sports people often talk about great comebacks, about people who were injured or fell far behind or dropped to a lower level of play and then came roaring back to triumph against great odds right at the end of the game or the season. But there is no comeback that can equal a child of God who has fallen or stumbled coming back to Jesus. Every time it happens, it is truly a miracle. There is more joy in heaven over a single spiritual comeback than over a hundred Superbowl rings! The greatest comeback in history is any child of God who, like Peter, faces whatever it takes to come back to God. If you find yourself in need of such a comeback, the last part of this lesson and this unit is especially for you.

 **Journaling**
(Experience)

Is there some pain that I am going through right now that is really a growth experience being directed by God?

What to Do When You've Blown It Spiritually

Any relationship with Jesus will tend to have its ups and downs. There are times of tremendous joy and spiritual strength. Then you stumble into an old sin and, like Peter, start questioning whether Jesus could possibly accept you anymore. Satan keeps throwing that sin in your face, trying to shatter your confidence in Christ.

What would Jesus have us do when we fall, when we blow it big time? What is the path to a full restoration of the joy of relationship with Jesus? How can we know that we are accepted in spite of what we have said, thought, or done?

1. Know what kind of God you are dealing with. What is God like? " 'For I know the plans I have for you,' declares the Lord, 'plans to prosper you and not to harm you, plans to give you hope and a future' " (Jeremiah 29:11). God is not like we are, sitting around thinking the worst about others. God's plans are plans to prosper us, not to destroy us. God is on our side. We see this God in the book of Jeremiah, planning seventy years ahead of time to deliver His unfaithful people and restore them to their land. We see this God in His incredible forgiveness of David, one of the great sinners of all time. We see Him in the Father who welcomes back the prodigal son. We see Him in the Man who looks up into a tree and invites Himself to Zacchaeus's house for dinner. We see Him in the Man who is the life of Matthew's party. We see a God who welcomes sinners, from Nicodemus to the Samaritan woman, from the most faithful of church members to the most jaded of criminals, from Jew to Gentile, from rich to poor.

When we've fallen back into sin, we must remind ourselves that God loves sinners! God forgives sinners! God accepts sinners, even before they ask sometimes. God gives sinners new life. The message here is not that sin doesn't matter; the message is: "No matter what you've done, you can start over today." Note the incredible text in 1 Timothy 1:15, 16:

> Here is a trustworthy saying that deserves full acceptance: Christ Jesus came into the world to save sinners—of whom I am the worst. But for that very reason I was shown mercy so that in me, the worst of sinners, Christ Jesus might display his unlimited patience as an example for those who would believe on him and receive eternal life.

You think you've been bad? Paul claimed that he was the ultimate sinner, the absolute worst. Did that remove his access to the grace and mercy of God? On the contrary! It was *for that very reason* (emphasis supplied) that he had received mercy from Jesus. Jesus picked him out as an example to show us how deep His mercy goes. It is at those very times when you feel the worst that you have the greatest claim on His mercy! The more you need Him, the more ready He is to make an example of you through His unlimited patience and mercy! *That's* the kind of God you are dealing with!

2. Tell the truth about yourself. The Bible calls this confession. Confession is simply facing reality and being honest with God about it. Confession is saying, "God, I agree with Your assessment that I am a sinner. I agree that what I did was wrong, no excuses." Confession is about taking responsibility for your actions. There may have been mitigating circumstances. You may have stumbled into it. But confession doesn't make excuses; it just looks truth in the eye and says, "I blew it! I chose to be inattentive. I chose to sin because it looked like fun. I chose to put myself in a place where accidents can happen. I lost focus on You."

Confession is about exposing darkness to the light. "Everyone who does evil hates the light, and will not come into the light for fear that his deeds will be exposed. But whoever lives by the truth comes into the light, so that it may be seen plainly that what he has done has been done through God" (John 3:20, 21). It can be very painful to expose our darkness to the light. Our sense of self-worth will rebel against the shock. But if we are grounded in the value that we have at the Cross, if we are conscious of the kind of God we are dealing with, we can move ahead with our confession, because not moving ahead leaves us feeling just as Peter did in his agony of remorse, guilt, and lost relationship.

3. Ask for forgiveness. It's that simple. There is no need for weeks and weeks of penance to show God just how sorry you really are. "*If we confess our sins*, he is faithful and just and will forgive us our sins and purify us from all unrighteousness" (1 John 1:9, emphasis supplied). God doesn't keep a scorecard of our wrongs; He doesn't keep throwing our mistakes in our faces. Satan does that. God doesn't stack up a bunch of conditions before He is willing to forgive.

Those conditions were already met in Jesus Christ. "For no matter how many promises God has made, they are 'Yes' in Christ" (2 Corinthians 1:20). We sometimes think God is not consistent, forgiving us when we feel good but tormenting us when we feel bad. In this text Paul insists that God is consistent; His answer to our requests for for-

God doesn't stack up a bunch of conditions before He is willing to forgive. Those conditions were already met in Jesus Christ.

giveness is always Yes!

The story is told that Martin Luther, the great German reformer, was once approached by the devil, who tried to discourage him with a list of his sins. Luther looked at the list and said, "That's not a complete list; you have more work to do." The devil returned later with a longer list. Luther looked at it again and said, "That's still not complete; you have more work to do." The devil returned again later with an even longer list. Luther looked at it carefully and said, "I think that is probably complete. Now I have something to say to you. The blood of Jesus cleanses us from *all* sin." And he picked up a bottle of ink that was nearby and threw it at the devil, smashing it against the wall (the ink blot remains on the wall of Wittenberg Castle to this day, touched up

158

for the sake of tourists). God loves to see that kind of holy boldness in us!

4. Plan to forsake that sin forever. Paul says, "Clothe yourselves with the Lord Jesus Christ, and do not think about how to gratify the desires of the sinful nature" (Romans 13:14). How can you do this when sin may even be fun at times? There are two answers. First, make a list. Total up some of the consequences of continuing in sin. Read the list to yourself every time you are tempted to sin. It can go a long way toward making that sin distasteful to you. Here's what such a list might look like.

For the sake of discussion, let's say your sin was sexual in nature. If you continue in sexual sin, you would probably become indecisive spiritually, never quite sure when and if you dare speak out for God. You could become secretive, constantly piling up ways to keep others from finding out. God will seem far away, you will have trouble praying, you will lose a sense of His approval and His presence. You will suffer guilt, which destroys your sense of self-worth. You will feel awful all the time, except when you are practicing your sin. You have a sense of regret, knowing that you have disappointed your Best Friend. You could develop difficulties in your marriage later on. And so on. . . . Are a few moments of pleasure worth all that? I DON'T THINK SO!

Second, if it's thrills that you are looking for, find some sin-free ways to pile up some thrills in your life. Take a sled sixty miles an hour down a snow-covered sand dune. Go backpacking into the wilderness with your best friend and conquer the elements, learning skills as you go. Go climb a serious mountain with a knife-edge or two to challenge you both mentally and physically. Take a trip or two to some exotic place. I'm sure you can think of a dozen ways to get thrills without the terrible side effects that sin brings.

Journaling
(Insight or Prayer)

What areas in my life need to go through these four steps?

Conclusion

There is absolutely nothing that can compare with the feeling that comes from being at peace with God, from being totally committed to His will. There is nothing like the joy that comes when your conscience is clean and there is nothing between you and God or between you and anybody else. Christianity has lasted two thousand years because nothing can compare with the kind of life that comes when you have a living relationship with Jesus Christ. It is possible to go through the motions and call it Christianity. It is possible to accept a do-and-don't religion as a substitute for the real thing. But the real thing is the greatest. Don't let anything keep you from it! You want the best. DON'T SETTLE FOR LESS!

Anchor Text

"Jesus did many other things as well. If every one of them were written down, I suppose that even the whole world would not have room for the books that would be written" (John 21:25).

Reaction

Discussion Questions

1. Why didn't Jesus spend more time with His disciples after His resurrection?

2. How could Peter feel hurt by Jesus' words and actions when he knew that Jesus was the Son of God? If you were asked the same question that Jesus asked Peter, how would you respond?

3. Is it possible to advance spiritually in times of prosperity and success? If so, how?

4. What is the purpose of public confession of sin? When is it not appropriate?

5. By moving the fish into the disciples' net, Jesus was acting as the second Adam, who had rule over the fish of the sea. What significance does this concept have for us today? In what ways are we still connected to the first Adam?

Expanded Horizons

1. For Bible Search 6 you were to provide the wording of the threefold conversation between Jesus and Peter. Read John 21:15-17 and then:
   A. Write a paragraph describing how you would feel if you had been in Peter's place.
   B. Write another paragraph stating what purpose such a conversation might have in your life right now.

2. John 21:20-23 is a very early reference to an effort on the part of some Christians to set an approximate time for the second coming of Jesus.

   A. In a paragraph or two write what you think "the brothers" were trying to accomplish by spreading this rumor and what the consequences would have been if John hadn't taken the time to squelch the rumor.

   B. Write a paragraph expressing how you relate or would relate to similar attempts to set a time for Jesus' coming.

161

Acknowledgments and Thanks

Grateful acknowledgment and recognition is given to those who made a valuable contribution to the development of the **John** unit of study.

SECONDARY BIBLE TEXTBOOK STEERING COMMITTEE

The following served on the Secondary Bible Textbook Steering Committee and were responsible for supervising the development of the Student Textbook, Teacher Edition and Teacher Resource Manual for the **John** unit of study:

Gerry E. Thompson, Chair, Director of Education, Pacific Union Conference
DeWayne Boyer, Bible Teacher, Takoma Academy
Cherry Lidner Habenicht, Bible Teacher, Wisconsin Academy
Gordon Kainer, Bible Teacher, Loma Linda Academy
Gerald Kovalski, Director of Education, Southern Union Conference
Glenn E. Russell, Bible Teacher, Andrews Academy

CONSULTANTS AND STAFF

The following provided valuable support services to the Steering Committee during the development of one or more components of the **John** unit.

Consultant

Don Weatherall, Assistant Director, North American Division Office of Education

Staff

Shirley Goodridge, editorial assistant and copyright authorizations
Beverly Benson, word processing of manuscripts for Student Textbook and Teacher Edition
Ardyce Weatherall, word processing of manuscripts for Teacher Resource Manual

WRITER

Jon Paulien, professor of New Testament, Theological Seminary, Andrews University, served as writer for the **John** unit. He brought a rich background of experiences as a college and seminary teacher of religion and a writing style that adds interest and variety in approaches to the topics covered.

TEACHERS AND STUDENTS

The teachers and students in the senior academies in the North American Division who field tested lessons in the **John** unit during the 1997–1998 school year. Their responses on the evaluation questionnaires provided valuable input and insights.

TEACHER RESOURCE MANUAL WORKSHOP COMMITTEE

Appreciation is extended to those teachers and other education personnel who served on the Teacher Resource Manual Workshop Committee for the **John** unit during the summer of 1998. The members were:

Don Weatherall, Chair, Assistant Director, North American Division Office of Education

Jan Fautheree, Bible Teacher, Gem State Adventist Academy

Gayle Norton, Bible Teacher, Walla Walla Valley Academy

Jynean Palmer Reid, Bible Teacher, Greater Atlanta Adventist Academy

Jan Yakush, Bible Teacher, College View Academy

PACIFIC PRESS® PUBLISHING ASSOCIATION

Paul Hey, liaison with the Secondary Bible Textbook Steering Committee

Bonnie Tyson-Flyn, in-house editor

DESIGN AND PAGE LAYOUT

GENESIS DESIGN/Bryan Gray, www.genesis-online.com

PUBLISHERS, AUTHORS, AND AGENTS

Grateful acknowledgment is made to the following publishers, authors, and agents for permission to use and adapt copyrighted materials:

Pacific Press® Publishing Association for the adaptation of the story in Lesson 10 from *The Lovely Lord of the Lord's Day* by Glenn and Ethel Coon. Copyright 1976. Used by permission.

All Scripture references not otherwise credited are from the Holy Bible: New International Version.

Every effort has been made to trace the ownership of all copyrighted material in this book and to obtain permission for its use.

Sincere appreciation is given to the many others who have contributed to the manuscript whose names may not be included.

PHOTO AND ILLUSTRATION CREDITS FOR JOHN

p. 12   Justinen Creative Group

p. 16   Darrel Tank

p. 20   Darrel Tank

p. 28   Tony Stone Images

p. 30   Review and Herald Publishing Assn.

p. 36   Nathan Greene

p. 38   Darrel Tank

p. 40   Review and Herald Publishing Assn.

p. 44   Nathan Greene

p. 52   Photodisc

p. 62   Weststock/Fotopic International

p. 64   Darrel Tank

p. 70   Justinen Creative Group

p. 80   Darrel Tank

p. 84   Marcus Mashburn

p. 88   International Stock

p. 96   Darrel Tank

p. 99   Review and Herald Publishing Assn.

p. 106   Justinen Creative Group

p. 109   Darrel Tank

p. 114   Digital Stock

p. 120   Bryan Gray

p. 126   Photodisc

p. 134   Justinen Creative Group

p. 136   Review and Herald Publishing Assn.

p. 140   Darrel Tank

p. 144   Darrel Tank

p. 152   Tony Stone Images

Cover illustration by Bryan Gray/Genesis Design. Images by Darrel Tank and Justinen Creative Group.